# 3D in Photoshop

# The Ultimate Guide for Creative Professionals

Zorana Gee
Pete Falco

AMSTERDAM ● BOSTON ● HEIDELBERG ● LONDON ● NEW YORK ● OXFORD
PARIS ● SAN DIEGO ● SAN FRANCISCO ● SINGAPORE ● SYDNEY ● TOKYO
Focal Press is an imprint of Elsevier

Focal Press is an imprint of Elsevier
The Boulevard, Langford Lane, Kidlington, Oxford, OX5 1GB, UK
30 Corporate Drive, Suite 400, Burlington, MA 01803, USA

First published 2010

**Notices**
Knowledge and best practice in this field are constantly changing. As new research and experience broaden our understanding, changes in research methods, professional practices, or medical treatment may become necessary.

Practitioners and researchers must always rely on their own experience and knowledge in evaluating and using any information, methods, compounds, or experiments described herein. In using such information or methods they should be mindful of their own safety and the safety of others, including parties for whom they have a professional responsibility.

To the fullest extent of the law, neither the Publisher nor the authors, contributors, or editors, assume any liability for any injury and/or damage to persons or property as a matter of products liability, negligence or otherwise, or from any use or operation of any methods, products, instructions, or ideas contained in the material herein.

**British Library Cataloguing in Publication Data**
3D in photoshop: the ultimate guide for creative professionals.
   1. Adope photoshop. 2. Digital art. 3. Three-dimensional imaging.
   I. Gee, Zorana. II. Falco, Pete.
   776-dc22

**Library of Congress Control Number:** 2010930199

ISBN: 978-0-240-81377-6

For information on all Focal Press publications
visit our website at focalpress.com

Printed and bound in the United States

10 11 12 10 9 8 7 6 5 4 3 2 1

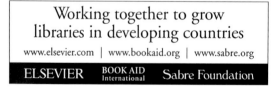

# Contents

# Contents

# Contents

# Foreword

Gavin Miller

Traditional analog photography combined the creative use of cameras with post processing in the darkroom. Photographers adjusted scene composition and lighting, and controlled exposure, focal length and depth of field to capture the moment on film. In the darkroom, chemical manipulation for transfer curves was combined with optical manipulations such as dodge and burn, convolutions using moving film (such as a Rostrum Camera) and compositing using optical masks.

Photoshop, in its early days, was largely inspired by the desire to move image manipulations to the digital realm in which they were more repeatable, convenient and expressive, allowing not dozens but hundreds of layers, and image transformations and effects not possible with analog processing. At the same time, Photoshop became a rich graphic design medium in which vector or raster graphics could be manipulated to create the impression of some simple forms of lighting and geometry, such as floating text with drop shadows and embossing.

With the growth of 3D functionality in Photoshop, the creative potential is expanding in a new direction, in which it is the photographic studio itself that becomes virtual, with lights, cameras and models taking the form of algorithms rather than physical objects. Many of the same creative decisions remain from physical photography such as scene composition and camera focal length and depth of field. But there are a range of new artistic decisions to make in which the models themselves can be made of a wide variety of shapes and materials. Images take on a new role as surface textures applied to geometry, capturing the appearance and structure of substances rather than whole objects.

A 3D rendering might be an end in itself, or be part of a larger composition with captured imagery or 2D graphic elements. By integrating 2D and 3D tools into the same application, a new creative medium is possible in which layer effects and 3D rendering styles interact to produce images that would be expensive or impossible to make with either alone. 3D graphics imposes a certain amount of structure on the resulting images, with shadows consistent with the geometry and lighting. Sometimes a designer will have a particular look in mind and carefully manipulate all the elements to produce the desired result, but just as valid is exploring the model by moving the camera and lights around until a happy accident of light and shadow resonate with the viewer, as happens with physical photography.

3D graphics has been seen in the past as difficult and expensive for a number of reasons. Firstly, the computational power required for high-quality image-making has only recently become main stream. Secondly, the creation of suitable 3D models is a large undertaking. Finally, there is a steep learning curve to high-end 3D production tools. The problem of model creation is being tackled in two ways. For many objects, models now exist in large libraries on the web, and using them for a particular purpose then becomes a matter of designing the textures and lighting for a given shot – something at which Photoshop excels. Secondly, Photoshop CS5 now has a new modeling tool called Repoussé that focuses on transforming 2D graphic designs, including text, into high-quality 3D models. While this does not solve the general modeling problem, it does make accessible the creation of graphic designs with embedded 3D elements that rival high-end packages. Combined with imported models and 2D visual elements, highly professional images are possible with a reasonable amount of work.

For photographers interested in learning how their real-world skills might extend to graphic design, or for graphic designers keen to grow their 2D talents into a world of depth and light, this book should serve as a good introduction. Early chapters focus on the elements of 3D image-making and how to control them in Photoshop CS5. Later chapters introduce model creation using Repoussé, and then take on the form of tutorials in which experts in the field explore how to combine the best features of 2D and 3D graphics. After that, the readers should be well position to explore the creative potential of this new tool.

# About the Authors and Acknowledgements

This book was a collective effort by the Adobe Photoshop 3D Team along with the Department of Procedural Imaging in Adobe's Advanced Technologies Lab and, of course, our amazing 3D designers and artists – Bert Monroy, Corey Barker, Russell Brown and Stephen Burns.

Listed below are the authors and contributors from the Photoshop 3D Team:

**Zorana Gee** is a Photoshop Product Manager and has been on the team for over 10 years. She has been involved with Photoshop Extended from the beginning and is instrumental in the 3D effort. Zorana holds an MBA from SCU Leavey School of Business. She speaks world-wide on Photoshop and Extended and has a deep understanding of the whole product.

**Pete Falco** is our Lead Photoshop 3D Engineer and a contributing author. He is also the co-editor of this book. Pete received his Masters in Engineering from Rensselaer Polytechnic Institute and has over 15 years of experience in the fields of 3D and image processing. He has been on the Photoshop team for 5 years and prior to that was an engineer on QuickTime VR, RealSpace, and Live Picture, and was a co-founder of Zoomify.

**Daniel Presedo** is a Photoshop 3D Quality Engineer as well as the primary artist for many of the images in Parts I and II of this book. He has worked professionally in the illustration and desktop publishing fields since 1992. With his unique skill set and proficiency in many 3D applications from Poser to 3D Max, he helps to influence how Photoshop 3D features are delivered.

**Nikolai Svakhine** is a computer scientist on the Photoshop team and a contributing author to this book. With M.S. from Moscow State University (1999) and Ph.D. from Purdue University (2007), he joined Adobe Systems in early 2007. His expertise includes OpenGL advanced surface and volume rendering, stereo/lenticular rendering and distributed network rendering.

**Mark Maguire** is a Photoshop 3D Engineer and a contributing author. Mark received his Bachelors in Computer Science from the University of Massachusetts at Amherst and has been in the 3D, video and gaming field for 16 years. He has been on the Photoshop team for 5 years at Adobe and also worked on the LiveMotion team. Prior to Adobe, he worked on a video editing software and award-winning children's games.

In addition, we had two contributing authors from Adobe's Advanced Technologies Lab:

**Pushkar Joshi** is a researcher in the Advanced Technology Labs at Adobe and is one of the developers of the Repoussé modeling system in Photoshop. His research interests include geometric modeling, intuitive interfaces for 2D and 3D design, animation, and information visualization. He studied variational shape design for his Ph.D. under Carlo Sequin at U.C. Berkeley. Prior to Adobe, he held research internships at Pixar Animation studios and the Institute for Creative Technologies.

**Aravind Krishnaswamy** is a researcher in the Advanced Technology Labs at Adobe and is one of the developers of the Ray Tracer in Photoshop. His current research interests include the simulation and visualization of light interaction with matter. The results of his research on the interaction of light with human skin have been presented to the community in various publications and tutorials (SIBGRAPI, Eurographics, AFRIGRAPH and SIGGRAPH Asia). He recently co-authored a book titled *Light and Skin Interactions – Simulations for Graphics Applications*.

A special thanks goes out to Gavin Miller, Fellow Scientist, and Nathan Carr, Senior Computer Scientist, who are the primary developers, along with Aravind, for the Adobe Ray Tracer (ART).

I also want to thank Domnita Petri for being an awesome and thorough 3D Quality Engineer – always keeping the quality bar high and Tai Luxon for stepping in and helping as technical editor.

The following artists and designers wrote the workflow chapters in the book:

**Bert Monroy** is considered one of the pioneers of digital art. His work has been seen in many magazines and scores of books. He has served on the faculty of many well-known institutions, lectured around the world, written many books and appeared on hundreds of TV shows. Bert hosts a weekly podcast called *Pixel Perfect* for Revision3.com. He co-authored *The Official Adobe Photoshop Handbook*, the first book on Photoshop, plus many other books since. His latest book, *Photoshop Studio with Bert Monroy: Digital Painting*, has received critical acclaim around the world. Bert writes a column for *Photoshop User* and *Layers* magazines.

**Corey Barker** is a content developer for Kelby Media Group and Executive Producer of the popular tutorial site Planet Photoshop. He is also co-host of the hit podcast *Layers TV* and makes occasional appearances on Photoshop User TV. Corey is also the co-author of the recent *Photoshop CS4 Down & Dirty Tricks* book and a featured instructor for the Down & Dirty Tricks seminar tour. Corey has also taught at events like Photoshop World and Adobe MAX.

**Stephen Burns** has been a corporate instructor and lecturer in the application of digital art and design for the past 10 years. He has been exhibiting digital fine art internationally at galleries such as Durban Art Museum in South Africa, Citizens Gallery in Yokahama, Japan, and CECUT Museum Of Mexico to name a few. Part of his exhibiting won him 1st place in the prestigious Seybold International digital arts contest. He also teaches Digital Manipulation workshops in San Diego and is the author of several books published by Charles River media.

**Russell Preston Brown** is the Senior Creative Director at Adobe Systems Incorporated as well as an Emmy award-winning instructor. His ability to bring together the world of design and software development is a perfect match for Adobe products. In Russell's 24 years of creative experience at Adobe, he has contributed to the evolution of Adobe Photoshop with feature enhancements, advanced scripts, and, most recently, Flash panel development.

# Introduction

This book is the first of its kind that covers all things 3D in Photoshop CS5 Extended. It is written by the Adobe Photoshop 3D team themselves as well as respected Photoshop industry leaders and educators. The book has two overall objectives – to provide the ultimate reference guide for any creative professional new to 3D as well as to provide creative and inspiring tutorials that will walk you through the how-to of working with 3D in Photoshop CS5 Extended.

Part I covers general 3D concepts that are important to understand before experimenting and designing with 3D. Part II covers how 3D works in Photoshop CS5 Extended, including many of the useful features and workflows important for any creative professional. Part III inspires us with awesome 3D tutorials by known Photoshop educators and designers. Part IV covers important file format information as well as information about interoperability.

I hope this book will entice all designers to explore the benefits and awe that 3D can bring into their designs and, most importantly, learn something new while having fun!

# PART I

# Introduction to 3D Concepts

## In this part

This book is all about Photoshop and the ways you can integrate 3D into your design workflows; however we wanted to take a step back and start off with an introduction to basic 3D concepts that will be important to understand, before diving into how it all works in Photoshop. In this part we explain 3D concepts in a way that anyone new coming into the world of 3D can understand so that they can have a solid framework to begin exploring. Further, those of you that are already familiar with 3D can learn about the different techniques that we use and how these can add to or optimize your existing workflows.

# CHAPTER 1

# Scene

## 1.1. The 3D Scene

A typical 3D scene has several elements which generate a scene when combined. You can think of setting up a 3D scene in the same way you would set up a photography studio (image above). First, you will need something to take a picture of (your meshes). Second, these meshes will have materials on them such as wood, cotton, or metal. Third, you need to provide lighting to the scene with one or more lights. And finally, you need a camera to take the picture with (rendering). The term rendering is the act of taking a picture of your scene through your virtual camera using the lighting, material and meshes you have set up.

## 1.2. Meshes and Vertices

### 1.2.1. 3D vs 2D

So, what exactly is 3D? You may recall from doing graphing in high school algebra. You would have two values (x and y) and then find their positions along the x and y axis of a graph and then use these positions to plot a point. If you made three of these points and connected them, you would have a triangle. If you extend this by adding a third axis (z), you can plot points anywhere in three-dimensional space to create 3D shapes (Figure 1.1).

3D in Photoshop. DOI: 10.1016/B978-0-240-81377-6.10001-8

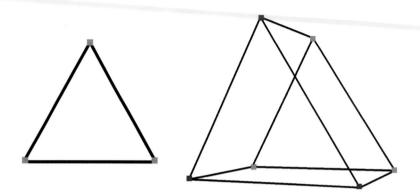

**FIG 1.1** A triangle consists of three points on two dimensions (x and y). Extending this to a third axis (z axis) results in a triangle in 3D.

Objects in a 3D scene are described as collections of 3D points, which are called vertices. These vertices are collected into groups of three, which form triangles. These triangles are contained in groups called meshes. Prior to the time that these triangles are actually drawn, meshes can be described in many different ways. For example, the equation for a sphere represents a 3D object. However, if it is to be drawn, it must first be broken down into an approximation of this shape using triangles (Figure 1.2).

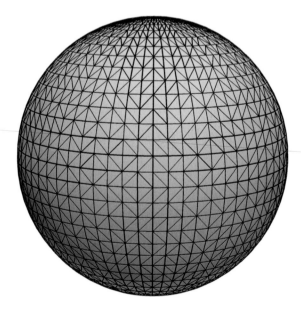

**FIG 1.2** A sphere represented by triangles, used to define meshes.

## 1.3. Cameras

There are two types of camera supported by Photoshop — orthographic and perspective. Both kinds of cameras have a location, or where the camera is located in 3D coordinates, and a direction that it is pointed.

### 1.3.1. Perspective Camera

A perspective camera behaves like a "real world" camera. Perspective cameras also have a lens, which has a "zoom" that can be represented as a field of view in degrees or a focal length in mm. This kind of lens will have perspective distortions as you increase or decrease the field of view.

### 1.3.2. Orthographic Camera

An orthographic camera is mostly used in engineering and architecture — as well as in the 3D modeling process. This type of camera has no perspective distortion which means that when moved, the object of interest does not change size or shape. This can be very useful when you are trying to align things in 3D space. Orthographic cameras have a scale, which represents the size of the slice it cuts through the 3D space. One thing of note here is that with an orthographic camera, moving an object further from or closer to the camera (or moving the camera) results in no change to the rendering whereas with a perspective camera, this will change the way things look dramatically (Figure 1.3).

**FIG 1.3** The top row shows a perspective camera where the car in the middle that is closer to the camera appears to be larger than the car that is farther away from the camera. The bottom row shows an orthographic camera where both cars regardless of distance from the camera, appear to be the same size.

### 1.3.3. Depth of Field

In addition to the position and direction of the camera, Photoshop CS5 can also simulate the aperture of the camera. This is done using the depth of field settings. With these, you specify the part of your scene that is in focus and that which is not — in much the same way you focus a lens on a subject when taking a photograph (Figure 1.4a).

**FIG 1.4a** Depth of Field set so that the front of the truck is in focus (the plane of focus) and everything else in front of or behind this plane is out of focus.

In Photoshop CS5, cameras have a pair of new parameters that allow an artist to control depth of field. The Distance control determines the plane in the scene where everything is in focus and the Blur control determines how out of focus the areas behind and in front of the focus plane are (Figure 1.4b).

**FIG 1.4b** With the Camera Zoom Tool selected, you can set the distance of the focal plane and the amount of blur.

## 1.4. Lights

Visual perception is our perception of how light interacts with matter. Therefore lighting is a key component of a 3D scene, similar to the importance of lighting in photography. Generally, light interaction with an object is a very complicated process. Though the primary intent for 3D rendering is to reproduce the light interaction with materials, steps are taken to simplify and approximate these calculations. One such step is to limit the supported types of light sources.

In Photoshop CS5, four types of light sources are supported. The first three are standard lights that can be found, in one form or another, within any 3D rendering package (point, infinite and spot lights).

### 1.4.1. Point Light

In some applications, this also may be known as an "omni" light. A point light is a light source emitting light equally in all directions. You can think of this like a candle or a light bulb. These types of lights have position, but do not have a direction (Figure 1.5).

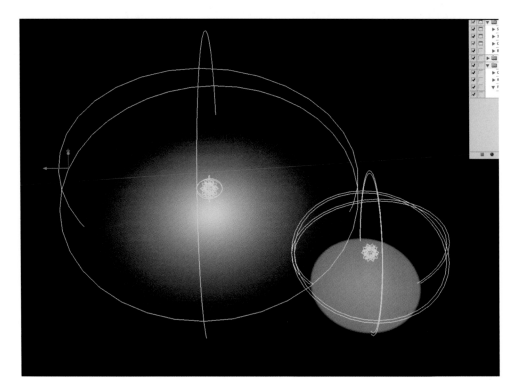

**FIG 1.5** A point of light depicted by a spherical widget.

## 1.4.2. Infinite Light

In some applications, this also may be known as a "directional" light. An infinite light is a light source emitting light parallel to a certain direction. This is useful for simulating light sources that are very far away (e.g., sunlight). These types of lights have direction, but do not have a defined position (Figure 1.6).

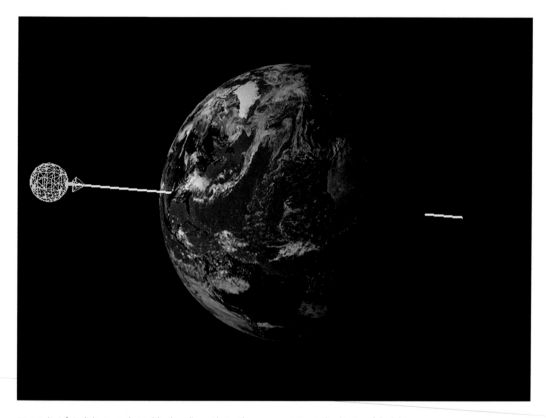

**FIG 1.6** An infinite light source depicted by the yellow widget with an arrow pointing in the direction of the light source.

## 1.4.3. Spot Light

Spot lights are similar to photographic spotlights or automobile headlights. These lights have defined positions, direction, and a hotspot angle (Figure 1.7).

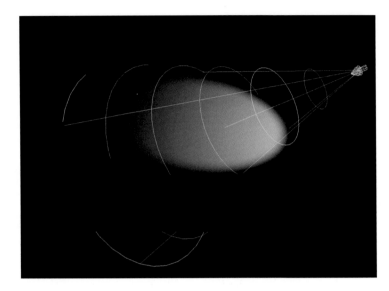

FIG 1.7 A spot light depicted by the widget pointing in the direction of the light.

### 1.4.4. Image-Based Light

An image-based light in Photoshop CS5 provides an "environment" light source, where the light source is not a point or a beam, but a texture map, spherically wrapped around your scene (spherical panorama). One way to imagine such a light is to think of it as a set of tiny point lights mounted on the spherical cage all around your scene where every point light corresponds to a single pixel in your texture map. In natural scenes, objects are rarely illuminated by simple light sources only. For example, if we consider an object within an empty room with a single lamp on the ceiling, while the lamp provides most of the lighting (called "direct" lighting), some of the light from the lamp gets reflected off the walls and back at the object (called "indirect" lighting). Similarly, an object in an outside scene is illuminated not only by the sun, but also by the sky and the ground. Thus, an image-based light greatly facilitates modeling of real-world lighting environments. Instead of approximating every light in your scene with a basic light source, you can now just use an image-based light textured with a spherical panorama, which is usually much easier to create (Figure 1.8).

## 1.5. Materials

Materials define the appearance of the object. These parameters include diffuse (main color), specularity (highlights), transparency, reflectivity and more. This derives from the notion that by setting all the properties in a given way, one can create the impression that the rendered object is made of some recognizable substance, like plastic, metal or glass. Materials often contain textures (Figure 1.9).

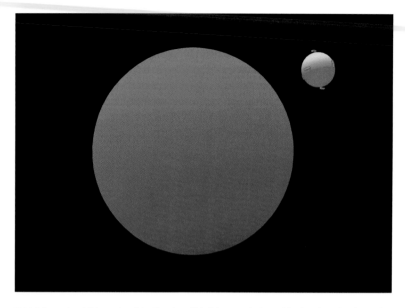

**FIG 1.8** Image-based light used to light this sphere. This light source is depicted by the spherical widget with the image wrapped around it and handles that allow you to rotate the map and reposition the lighting.

**FIG 1.9** Sample materials found in Photoshop CS5 Materials Library presets.

## 1.5.1. Photoshop-Supported Material Properties

Most Photoshop material properties have a base value (either a color or a single value) and a map. If a map is not specified, the base value is used across the entire surface of the material. If a map is specified, the values in the map override the base value. The alpha channel in the map is then used to blend (multiply) the value at each pixel in the map against the base value.

### Diffuse

The diffuse color is the color that an object reflects when illuminated by "good lighting," that is, by direct daylight or artificial light that makes the object easy to see (Figure 1.10). The color looks the same from all directions, similar to matte paint (highlights and reflections both depend on the direction from which you view the surface).

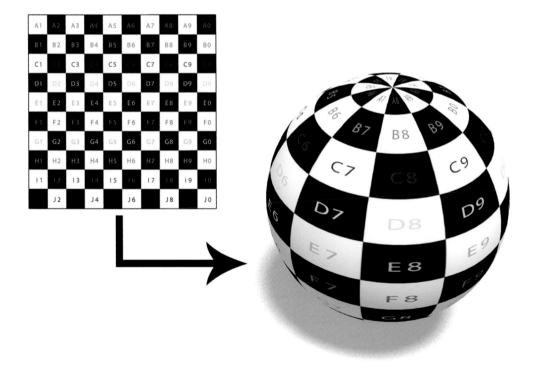

**FIG 1.10** The image on the left is a diffuse map of a checkerboard pattern which is wrapped around a 3D sphere. Where each pixel on the left corresponds to a position on the sphere.

FIG 1.11 This 3D model of a soda can has the background image set as its environment map with reflections on (reflection value > 0).

### Environment

Similar to the image-based light mentioned earlier, an environment map specifies colors on a sphere that wrap around your entire scene. In the case of the environment map, these colors are used for reflections (Figure 1.11).

### Bump Maps

Bump mapping makes an object appear to have a bumpy or an irregular surface (Figure 1.12). When you render an object with a bump-mapped material, lighter (whiter) areas of the map appear to be raised (pulled forward), and darker (blacker) areas appear to be pushed back.

### Opacity Maps

You can select an image to make an object partially transparent. Lighter (higher-value) values render as more opaque, darker areas render as more transparent — exactly the same as the way Opacity works in the Photoshop Layers panel (Figure 1.13).

### Shininess/Glossiness Maps

Shininess and glossiness control specular highlights. Shininess is the intensity or brightness of the highlights and glossiness is the size or spread of the highlight. Therefore, shininess needs glossiness to be used as an effect whereas glossiness does not need shininess (Figure 1.14). Using a map for glossiness will alter where the highlights appear on your model. Using a map for shininess will alter how bright the highlights appear on your model.

**Notes**: If an environment map is not specified for a material, and an image-based light is, the color in the image-based light will be used for reflections by default.

With reflections set to 0, you will not see the effect of an environment map since it won't have anything — object or surface — to bounce off of.

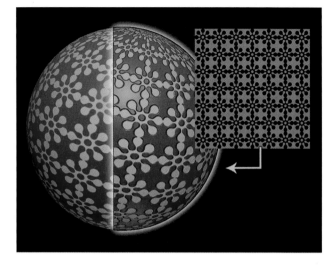

**FIG 1.12** This sphere shows the left side without a bump map and the right side with a bump map of this texture applied. The bump map is the grayscale image on the right where the color values determine if pixels are raised or pushed back.

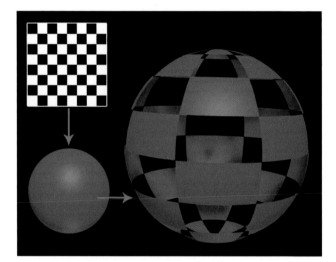

**FIG 1.13** The right sphere shows the checkerboard texture applied as an opacity map The color values in the texture map shown in the upper left corner determines how transparent that part of the object will be where black is fully transparent.

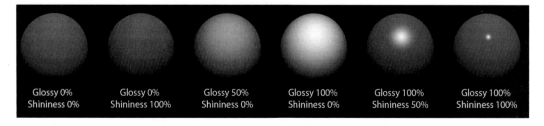

| Glossy 0% | Glossy 0% | Glossy 50% | Glossy 100% | Glossy 100% | Glossy 100% |
| Shininess 0% | Shininess 100% | Shininess 0% | Shininess 0% | Shininess 50% | Shininess 100% |

**FIG 1.14**   Effects from different parameters of Glossiness and Shininess applied.

FIG 1.15 Self-illumination can give lighting effects similar to this neon glow or the lighting you get from lava.

## Self Maps

Self-illumination is added to the color computed from diffuse, highlight and reflection shading. It can be thought of as luminous paint added to the total color and is independent of lighting (Figure 1.15). Another way to think of this effect is how lava is self-illuminated with the color red. You can use self-illuminated materials on objects that represent lights to simulate things like car headlights, and so on. White provides the most illumination, while black blocks the illumination completely. It's often a good idea to design a self-illumination map to match your diffuse map. For example, the diffuse map might have small, yellow rectangles to represent windows, while the self-illumination map consists of matching white rectangles against black to illuminate the yellow windows.

## Normal Maps

Normal Maps are textures used for simulating the lighting of bumps and dents on a 3D object — the direction in which a surface faces. It allows the program to add more detail to the 3D model without adding more polygons and thus creating a larger model and file. It is especially useful for real-time display devices such as game engines, and it can also be used in rendered scenes and animations. Photoshop's normal maps are object space normal maps. This means the RGB values in the texture are interpreted as a direction in space (x, y and z, respectively).

Often, normal maps are used to improve the render quality of a model with a low number of polygons (Figure 1.16). A game designer, for example, might make a low polygon-count version of a model that they have. They will then use the high polygon-count version of the model to generate a normal map and then apply that normal map to the low polygon-count version of the model.

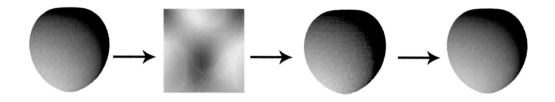

**FIG 1.16** Normal map applied to a low poly-count model to improve render quality. The shape on the far left shows a high poly-count model. The second image on the left shows the actual normal map. The third image on the left shows a low poly-count model without this normal map and the furthest image on the right shows this same low poly-count model with normal map applied, resulting in an improved render quality.

### Reflection/Refraction Maps

Reflection is how much light bounces off of an object. For example, chrome is a highly reflective material and light in the scene will have a strong reflection off the surface. Refraction defines how light behaves once it enters an object — and therefore requires some amount of transparency to have any effect (Figure 1.17). For example, looking through a ball made of glass has a different effect than looking through a ball made of diamond.

**Note**: See Chapter 2 for more on refraction.

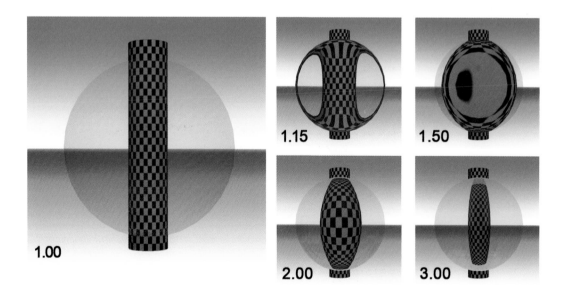

**FIG 1.17** A transparent sphere will have different effects when looking through it based on what the refraction index (R.I.) is.

## 1.6. UVs

UVs facilitate the placement of image texture maps on a 3D surface (Figure 1.18). They exist to define a two-dimensional texture coordinate system, called UV texture space. UVs are essential in that they provide the connection between the surface of the mesh and how the image texture gets mapped onto it. Basically, UVs act as marker points that control which points (pixels) on the texture map correspond to which points (vertices) on the mesh. Textures cannot be applied to surfaces that do not possess UV texture coordinates. UV texture space uses the letters U and V to indicate the axes in 2D instead of x and y since x and y are used for the 3D positions of the vertices.

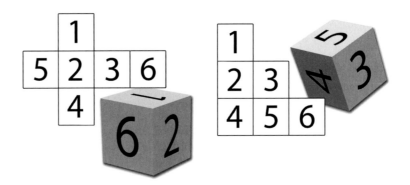

**FIG 1.18** These two die have different UV maps applied to them. The UV map will determine how the numbers (or image) are wrapped around the die.

In most cases, you map and arrange UVs after you have completed your modeling and before you assign textures to the model. Otherwise, changing the model will create a mismatch between the model and the UVs, and affect how any textures appear on the model.

Understanding the concept of UVs and how to map them to a surface, and subsequently lay them out accurately, is essential for producing textures on surfaces when working in any 3D program. Understanding how UVs work is also important when you want to paint on a 3D model. For example, if you paint a stroke on a single face of a die, the paint may in fact replicate on each respective face if the UV mapping dictates that the texture is tiled.

## 1.6.1. UV Maps

Adding 2D images to the surfaces of 3D objects provides a great way to decorate them. This process is known as texture mapping. Imagine placing a sticker onto a side of a bottle. The sticker represents the 2D image for decorating the surface. The necessary step is to determine where the sticker should go. This is a "mapping" from some location on the sticker to some place on the surface. Rather than mapping sticker locations onto the surface, it is more convenient to map locations on the surface onto locations of the sticker. This allows the pattern of the sticker to be repeated if desired across the surface of the bottle. This mapping from points on the mesh (e.g. bottle) into positions on the decal sticker (e.g. image) is known as a "UV mapping"

Many models may come with an existing UV map. If not, Photoshop will automatically UV map your models so that you can decorate them and paint them from start. The way in which Photoshop maps your models is to divide your object up into smaller pieces that can be squished flat. These flattened pieces are then packed into different locations of your image. When you paint or apply detail on that part of your 2D image, the colors show up on the respective part of the 3D model.

This mapping from 2D image locations to locations on the 3D model can be very confusing at first. Fortunately, in many cases you don't have to worry much about the UV mapping. By painting directly in 3D onto the surface of the model and Photoshop will automatically place any painted detail into the right corresponding place in the 2D texture. It may be necessary to start with a little painting in 3D before attempting to paint directly into the 2D image so that you can get your bearings on which parts of the image map to which parts of the surface.

The UV mapping process results in a correlation between the image and how it appears as a texture when mapped onto the three-dimensional surface mesh. UV mapping is a critical skill to master for accurate and realistic textures on polygonal surfaces.

Photoshop CS5 Extended does not provide any tools for doing UV mapping. Any models created from scratch in Photoshop will have UV coordinates assigned and any models that are loaded from external sources that do not have UV coordinates will have them assigned automatically if you wish to have more control over how these UVs get assigned, there are third party applications to allow you to do this.

**Note**: Although Photoshop CS5 Extended does not have any real control over UV mapping, you can edit the properties of the material and offset and scale the UV coordinates (Figure 1.19).

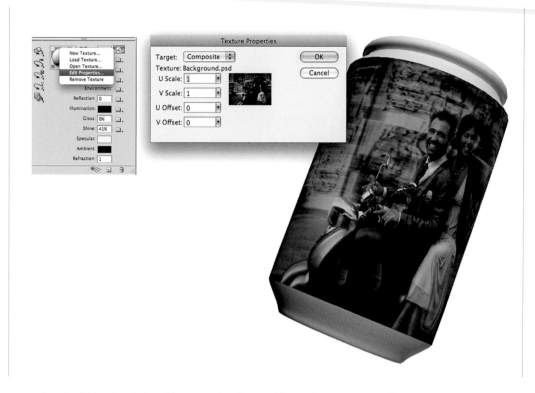

**FIG 1.19** From the 3D Material panel, choose Edit Properties from the material fly-out and you can scale and offset the texture coordinates.

# CHAPTER 2

# Rendering: OpenGL (OGL) and Adobe Ray Tracer (ART)

Rendering is the process of producing the pixels of an image from a higher-level description of its components. Photoshop CS5 Extended supports two different kinds of rendering — OpenGL and Ray Tracing. OpenGL rendering is used for the Interactive (Painting) mode, which is very fast, but lacks advanced rendering effects such as shadows, irradiance, inter-reflections, anti-aliasing, high quality depth of field, and full HDR rendering. Even though many modern high-end graphics cards are able to support some of those advanced features, the intent to support a wide variety of mid and low-end cards led to the decision that those features would only be supported by the Ray Tracer. Thus, the OpenGL-supported effects are a subset of Ray Tracer-supported effects, a trade-off for much faster rendering speeds necessary for interaction and smooth 3D workflows (Figure 2.1).

## 2.1. OpenGL

OpenGL (Open Graphics Library) is a cross-platform graphics rendering API. The main reason it is widely used is because many graphics cards or GPUs

**3D in Photoshop. DOI: 10.1016/B978-0-240-81377-6.10002-X**

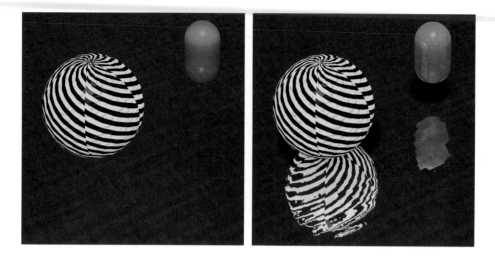

FIG 2.1 The image on the left shows GL rendering and the image on the right shows Ray Tracer rendering (support for extra effects).

(Graphics Processing Units, used by graphics cards) support extremely efficient hardware acceleration of OpenGL, which makes it an attractive solution for interactive graphics rendering. The basic GPU architecture, however, only allows for a certain set of rendering calculations, which results in a limited number of visual effects.

Since the GPU mass-market introduction in the mid-1990s, the set of supported calculations has been gradually expanding and the GPU programming interfaces have become more flexible. Because the driving force of GPUs is video game acceleration, one can trace the history of GPU capabilities by just looking at the effects you see in high-end video games over the different years. Even though GPUs have come a long way since their inception, their basic architectural limitations make certain rendering effects, such as shadows and radiosity, hard to implement (i.e., slow and/or memory intensive).

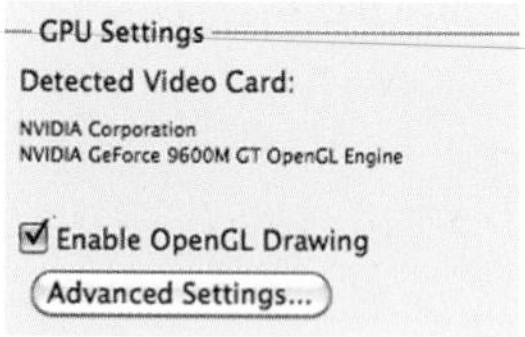

**GPU Settings**

Detected Video Card:

NVIDIA Corporation
NVIDIA GeForce 9600M GT OpenGL Engine

☑ Enable OpenGL Drawing

Advanced Settings...

FIG 2.2 OGL-enablement checkbox in the Performance section of Photoshop Preferences.

There are many 3D features that are dependent on the GPU in order to function, it is required that you use a video card that has at least 512MB of vRAM and supports OGL. 3D features that rely on OGL support are: Adobe Repoussé, all overlays (progressive rendering tiling, 3D Axis, Lights, Meshes, ground plane), Interactive/Painting rendering mode*, performance optimizations (auto-hide layers and direct-to-screen) and Image Based Lights. To check if OGL is enabled on your machine, navigate to Performance section in your Preferences (Figure 2.2). If this option is disabled on your system, check Photoshop system requirements and also be sure that the driver for your video card is up to date. For further trouble-shooting, navigate to Help > GPU in the Photoshop menu bar and/or check with your video card manufacturer.

---

* There is a software fallback (Ray Tracer) for the Interactive (Painting) rendering mode when OGL isn't enabled but performance is significantly reduced.

## 2.2. Ray Tracing

Ray tracing is a specific rendering approach in 3D computer graphics, which uses a technique that follows rays from the camera outward. It produces results similar to other techniques such as ray casting and scan line rendering, but facilitates more advanced optical effects, such as reflection and refraction, and is still efficient enough to be of practical use when high quality output is desired.

Ray tracing is a technique which simulates the paths that light takes in the real world as it starts from a light source, interacts with surfaces in the scene and finally lands on the sensor of a camera. In the ray tracing algorithm, we reverse these steps. For each pixel of our final image, we fire rays into the scene. When those rays hit an object, the color is evaluated by the material properties of the object at which point we fire more rays from the object to the various light sources and to other objects. With ray tracing, it is straightforward to faithfully reproduce such effects as hard and soft shadows, color bleeding, reflection, refraction and depth of field. If one fires an inadequate number of rays for each pixel in the image, then the resulting image will contain jagged edges (called aliasing) and will be quite noisy (Figure 2.3).

FIG 2.3  The scene on the left is rendered with a low quality (draft) Ray Trace mode and on the right is rendered with a high quality (final) Ray Trace mode.

To overcome this noise (aliasing), dozens to hundreds of rays are fired for each pixel. However, this can be very time-consuming — taking several minutes to hours with a very large document. The Ray Tracer in Photoshop CS5 uses a technique called progressive rendering, which continuously renders the image with a small number of rays per pixel. Photoshop then combines the results of the current pass with previous results to progressively improve the rendered result. As such, the first few passes can contain noticeable noise. However, showing this noisy image is intended to provide the artist with a good idea of the lighting and where shadows will be cast.

FIG 2.4 High Quality Threshold setting found in the Preferences for 3D settings.

The progressive rendering can be interrupted at any time to make scene changes. If it is accidentally interrupted, the rendering can be continued without starting over by using the Resume Progressive Render command found in the 3D menu as well as the 3D Panel fly-out.

Photoshop will also stop rendering portions of the image that it has detected are sufficiently noise free. A portion of the image is considered done when its noise gets below a given threshold. This threshold is controlled by a Preference in the 3D preference pane (Figure 2.4).

## 2.2.1. Ray Tracing Effects

There are several effects which are either only present with ray tracing or are much more accurate when using ray tracing. Shadows are only visible when using ray tracing. All four of the light types are capable of casting shadows, including soft shadows. In addition to casting shadows onto objects in the scene, shadows can also be cast onto a ground plane and these shadows can vary in terms of softness and opacity (Figure 2.5).

Image-based lighting gives an artist the ability to use an image to simulate the lighting in a scene. 32-bit images are recommended for image-based lights since at this bit depth you have over 4 billion levels to describe the light, whereas with 8-bit images you are limited to only 256 levels of light (0–255). If you have a broad range of light and dark areas, typically 256 levels of light will not be enough.

With the Ray Tracer, you can also simulate effects such as reflection and refraction. The reflection amount is controlled by the reflectivity material

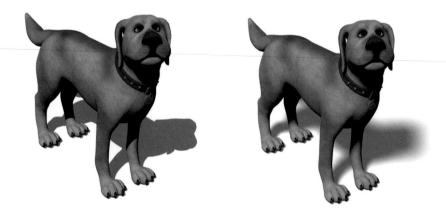

FIG 2.5 Image on the left has a hard shadow casting on the ground plane compared to the image on the right with a soft shadow.

parameter and the refraction amount is controlled by the opacity material parameter. The extent to which light rays are refracted is determined by the index of refraction. Water has an index of refraction of 1.33, glass 1.5 and diamond 2.4. See Table 2.1 for more common refraction indexes.

TABLE 2.1    Refractive Index for common materials. You can find the setting for this in the
3D Materials Panel (at the bottom of the panel).

| MATERIAL | INDEX |
|---|---|
| Vacuum | 1 |
| Air at STP | 1.00029 |
| Ice | 1.31 |
| Water at 20 C | 1.33 |
| Acetone | 1.36 |
| Ethyl alcohol | 1.36 |
| Sugar solution(30%) | 1.38 |
| Fluorite | 1.433 |
| Fused quartz | 1.46 |
| Glycerine | 1.473 |
| Sugar solution (80%) | 1.49 |
| Typical crown glass | 1.52 |
| Crown glasses | 1.52-1.62 |
| Spectacle crown, C-1 | 1.523 |
| Sodium chloride | 1.54 |
| Polystyrene | 1.55-1.59 |
| Carbon disulfide | 1.63 |
| Flint glasses | 1.57-1.75 |
| Heavy flint glass | 1.65 |
| Extra dense flint, EDF-3 | 1.72 |
| Methylene iodide | 1.74 |
| Sapphire | 1.77 |
| Rare earth flint | 1.7-1.84 |
| Lanthanum flint | 1.82-1.98 |
| Arsenic trisulfide glass | 2.04 |
| Diamond | 2.417 |

## 2.3. Other Render Settings

Ray Tracing and OGL are just two types of render modes. There are several other render settings in Photoshop CS5. We have created presets of these different types of settings that can be found in the 3D Scene Panel Render Settings menu (Figure 2.6); two of the more interesting ones are Depth Maps and Normal Maps.

FIG 2.6 Render Settings presets found in the 3D Scene panel.

### 2.3.1. Depth Map preset

Using the Depth Map render style, you can render an image where black represents the farthest point in the scene and white represents the closest point (Figure 2.7). The most effective way to use this render style is to render in using a 32-bit image with a Levels adjustment (to specify a narrow range of values). The adjustment layer is optional; however, it gives you an easier way to see what is going on and edit the map. 32-bits will give you a larger range of data to describe the depth, while with 8-bit images, you only have 256 levels of depth. With this map you can generate a smoother 3D object.

### 2.3.2. Normals preset

Photoshop CS5 also has a render style where the normals on the surface of the object are visualized (Figure 2.8). This can be useful when you are looking

**FIG 2.7** 3D object of a dog with its depth map on the right. White values indicate that those pixels will be the closest point and black values are the farthest.

**FIG 2.8** 3D object of a dog with its normal map on the right.

for "bad" normals. Bad normals can result in paint not being applied properly and incorrect renderings. (i.e. having holes in the paint applied). Normals that are bad will stick out since Photoshop ends up depositing paint incorrectly in a region of the mesh and you'll notice a color discontinuity. Usually the normals over a smooth surface results in continuous colors of the map, hence smooth transitions of colors on the object.

**Note**: For more information on normals see Chapter 1.

# 3D in Photoshop

## In this part

Now that you have a good foundation of basic 3D concepts from Part I of this book, we want to dive a little deeper and introduce all the 3D capabilities within Photoshop. In this part, we will cover how all the great 3D technologies are integrated into Photoshop and how to get started with the tools. You'll find that Photoshop is a logical place to begin learning about and using 3D in your designs, not only because Photoshop workflows are familiar but also because Photoshop allows you to leverage all the great 2D techniques that you already know into your 3D designs. There's a lot here so have fun!

# CHAPTER 3

# Getting Started with 3D in Photoshop

## 3.1. Workspace and the 3D Panel

When creating 3D designs, it is important to understand the complete workflow, as every step is critical in helping one complete and get to the final vision. The fundamental workflow is creating or obtaining the 3D model, adding/editing materials, adding/editing lights, adjusting shadows and other effects, and then finally rendering the scene. Of course, there will be quite a bit of back and forth between rendering your scene and re-adjusting the lights for optimal effects. Further, you can take your 3D layer and composite it with a 2D layer or add traditional 2D effects and touch-ups — one of the key benefits of working with 3D in Photoshop! This chapter will cover the essential things you need to know about working with 3D in Photoshop.

**Note**: For best performance, set your document up to screen resolution (72 ppi). If your final output is print, you can then scale up and re-render. This will optimize performance and speed when editing 3D.

3D in Photoshop. DOI: 10.1016/B978-0-240-81377-6.10003-1

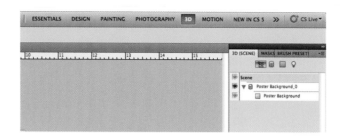

FIG 3.1 3D Workspace switcher. Select this workspace to open up necessary panels when working with 3D.

To get started, select the 3D workspace from the upper right corner of your application bar (Figure 3.1). This will open the important panels when working with 3D that will be referenced throughout the chapter.

With the 3D workspace selected, the panel in front view should be your 3D Scene panel (which you can also open from Windows > 3D). This panel has different views that dynamically update based on what component you have selected in your scene graph or in your Layers panel. The initial view will have controls that allow you to create or open 3D objects. This is described in further detail in the next section.

If you have a 3D layer selected, the 3D Scene panel has four active buttons, or filters, on the top of the panel (Figure 3.2). The first button shows you your scene graph, or scene components (meshes, materials and lights) as well as the scene properties you can edit. The second button filters out your meshes and lists out all the meshes in your 3D layer, or scene, as well as Mesh properties that you can edit. The third button filters out your materials and lists out all the materials in the scene as well as Material properties that you can edit. And lastly, the fourth button filters out your lights and lists out all the lights in your scene as well as the Light properties that you can edit. Each view of the panel and its associated properties will be discussed further in later sections.

FIG 3.2 3D Scene panel.

There are five tools sets on the left that are always available regardless of what view of the Scene panel you are in. These tools are movement tools for objects, cameras, meshes and lights as well as the Material Drop/Load Tool and the Select Material Tool. How to use these tools will be described in the following sections.

At the bottom of the panel there are three buttons. The first button on the left allows you to toggle overlays important for navigating around your 3D layer, or scene. These overlays are the 3D-Axis, Ground Plane, Lights and Selection. The button in the middle is used to create new lights (it will only be active with a light selected). The delete icon on the far right will delete whatever light you have selected in the scene graph.

**Note**: Overlays are dependant on OpenGL. Be sure that you have this option on in the Performance section of your Preferences.

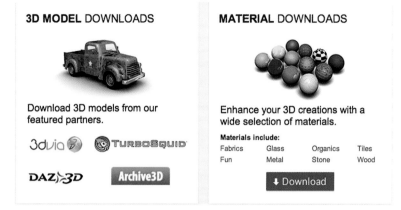

FIG 3.3  3D partner links and download for additional Material presets.

## 3.2. Importing 3D

You can either download models from 3D content providers and open them directly in Photoshop or create your own 3D models. There are many 3D content providers that have objects supported by Photoshop. It is recommended to work with Collada (dae) files but Photoshop also supports OBJ, KMZ, U3D and 3DS. For more information on format specifics, see Appendix A: File Formats. The easiest way to access these partner websites is by opening up the link found in the 3D menu under the command "Browse 3D Content Online… ." This will bring you to a 3D landing page with useful links and content.

This book includes a plugin created by 3D Via that allows you to import 3D objects directly from their warehouse into Photoshop CS4 or CS5 Extended. You can download this plugin from www.3D-in-Photoshop.com or directly from http://www.3dvia.com/photoshop (Figure 3.3).

## 3.3. Converting to 3D

Creating 3D has never been easier since the introduction of 3D in Photoshop. There are five ways now in Photoshop CS5 Extended to create real 3D geometries. You can access the commands to create 3D from the 3D menu or start from the 3D Scene panel Figure 3.4.

### 3.3.1. 3D Postcard

The easiest way to create 3D is by taking a layer and generating a 3D plane, or postcard (Figure 3.5). With the Selected Layer(s) set as your Source, choose 3D Postcard and Photoshop will create a 3D plane based on the pixels in your

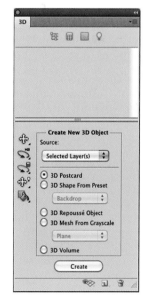

FIG 3.4  3D Scene panel: Panel view with 2D layer selected allowing you to create new 3D objects.

**31**

FIG 3.5   Converting a layer to a postcard.

layer. A postcard is also useful if you want to generate a plane to catch reflections, shadows, lighting, effects, etc. You can orient the plane perpendicular to your object and then merge the 3D objects together to a single layer. See Corey Barker's workflow in Chapter 9 for a tutorial on this.

## 3.3.2. 3D Shape from Preset

You can also take this layer and warp it around any 3D shape, or primitive, that Photoshop ships with. You can create your own 3D shape presets if you have a modeling application that exports Collada files. This is a great way to get started with basic 3D objects (Figure 3.6). See Bert Monroy's workflow in Chapter 8 for a tutorial on this.

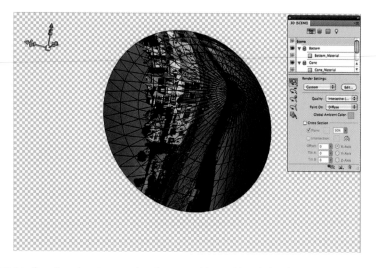

FIG 3.6   Converting a layer to a cone shape from presets (shown with a wireframe).

FIG 3.7 Converting a layer to a Repoussé object using the Type Mask Tool.

### 3.3.3. 3D Repoussé Object

You can take a selected layer (pixels, text or shape layers), selection or path and convert them to an Adobe Repoussé object (Figure 3.7). This feature allows you to extrude these layers to 3D geometry where many different extrusion parameters can be applied (i.e., twist, bend, bevel, inflate). For more information on creating Repoussé objects, see Chapter 7.

**33**

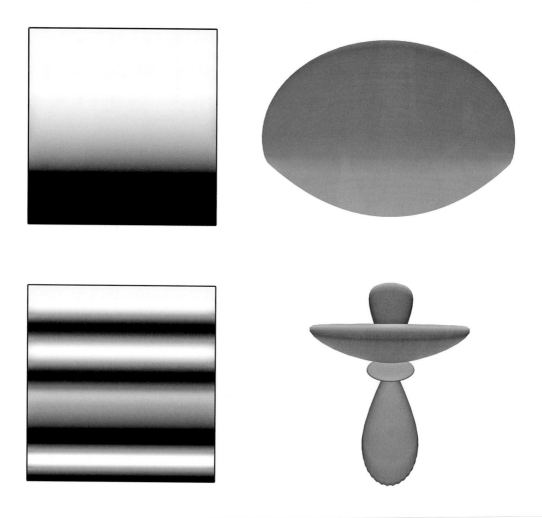

FIG 3.8 The images on the left are depth maps used to create the 3D objects on the right.

### 3.3.4. 3D Mesh from Grayscale

A 3D mesh can also be generated from a grayscale image, or map (Figure 3.8). Essentially, depth is determined by grayscale values where 50% gray is the starting plane and anything more black is pushed back and anything more white is pulled forward (in z-space). This is useful if you want to generate meshes with more precision; this is especially true if you use 16- or 32-bit images, since you now have pixel level control over the appearance of your mesh. Note that once created, you can open up your grayscale image and re-edit it and your mesh will be regenerated.

### 3.3.5. 3D Volumes

A 3D Volume is generated with two or more layers. The volume is an inter-
polation between layers and not real 3D geometry. This means that no mesh is
generated and you cannot apply many of the 3D capabilities to it. This is
primarily important for medical professionals working with DICOM images or
frames where viewing a volume rendering is useful. However, there are
interesting effects you can create by simply taking multiple layers (raster or
vector) and interpolating between the pixels to generate a volume (Figure 3.9).

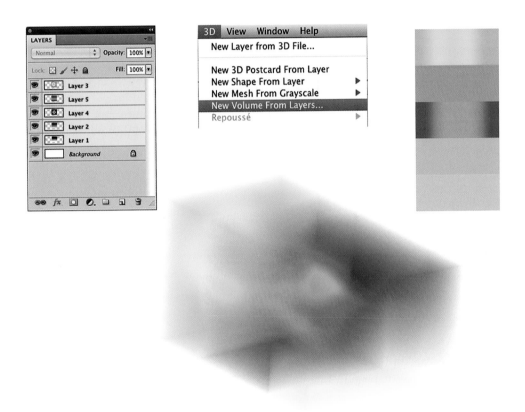

FIG 3.9  Image with five layers selected with a volume rendering from those five layers.

## 3.4. Navigating 3D

There are many 3D tools in Photoshop to help you manipulate your scene
components (objects, meshes, cameras and lights) as well as tools that help
with selecting and applying materials. The easiest way to manipulate positions of scene components is with the 3D-Axis Tool (Figure 3.10).

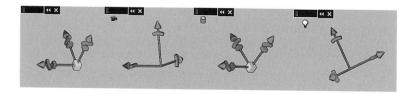

FIG 3.10  3D-Axis for objects, cameras, meshes and lights — upper left icon indicates component selected and pull on any handle to manipulate the object (i.e. roll, scale, pan, etc.).

With the 3D-Axis, you can rotate, roll, scale/pan, slide/walk 3D objects, meshes, lights and cameras depending on what tool you have selected in the toolbar or in the 3D Scene panel. An icon in the upper left of the 3D-Axis will indicate which component you are adjusting and the yellow handle will appear when adjustment that type of movement. You can make a variety of adjustments (rotate, roll, scale/pan, slide/walk) to the component you're manipulating without changing tools — simply by interacting with different parts of the 3D axis.

The 3D-Axis Tool is dependant on OGL. Be sure you have this option on in the Performance section of your Preferences.

You can also individually select scene component movement tools (i.e., Object Rotate, Camera Walk) from the toolbar, from the tools in the Scene panel or from the Options Bar of any 3D tool selected.

All tools can be assigned shortcuts. By default the 3D Object Rotation Tool has the keystroke K, and the Camera Rotation Tools have the keystroke N. Set custom shortcuts from Edit > Keyboard Shortcuts.

# CHAPTER 4

# Materials

Materials are important as they essentially define the appearance of the 3D object. Materials are made up of different properties that can be defined as a single value or a texture map that varies the value over the surface of the object. For a deeper dive on materials and what each property means, read Chapter 1: Section 1.5. Often, because materials are made up of different properties (i.e., bump, reflection, environment maps), you will need to render the 3D object using the Ray Tracer in order to see its full effect. See Chapter 2: Section 2.2 on Rendering with the Adobe Ray Tracer for more information.

3D objects often contain many materials. To view the materials that make up your 3D object, view the 3D Panel Materials filter to see a list (Figure 4.1). 3D objects are often divided into sections where each section can have a different material.

## 4.1. Material Library and Browsing Materials

Photoshop now has its own material library and presets. By default, Photoshop installs two sets of presets. One default set of materials is heavily

FIG 4.1 3D Materials Panel.

3D in Photoshop. DOI: 10.1016/B978-0-240-81377-6.10004-3

dependent on using the Ray Tracer to enable its effects. The other set is less dependent on the Ray Tracer as it inherently has less lighting properties. However, you will likely still get better output if you Ray Trace these as lighting set-up in the scene can also affect how the material will look. You can easily obtain more material presets by navigating to 3D > Browse 3D Content Online... from the application. Here you will find materials such as Metals, Fabrics, Organics, Tiles, Stone, and more. You can also save your created or edited materials as custom presets. From the fly-out menu of the Material browser (Figure 4.2), choose Save Material.

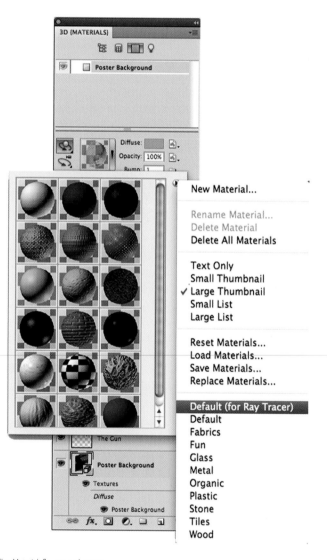

FIG 4.2 The Material fly-out and menu.

# 4.2. 3D Material Tools and Editing

To easily add any of the materials on to your 3D object, target the right Material from the list in the 3D Materials panel or use the Material Selector Tool 🔖 to select on canvas the material to target. Then, click on any material from the Material browser. The Material Selector Tool helps you to easily identify where in your scene graph the targeted material is (Figure 4.3).

**Note**: You can choose to turn on Selection overlay to see a boundary overlay around the selected material. The color of the overlay can be changed in the 3D section of your Preferences.

## 4.2.1. Material Dropper/Loader Tools

The Material Drop Tool 🔖 also serves as a Material Load Tool when using the Option/Alt key. It is a very important tool when editing materials as it allows one to load a material (with the Option/Alt key) and drop it onto any other part of the mesh or a different mesh within the scene, or on another layer. Alternately, you can load a material from your material presets by using the preset fly-out in the options bar (Figure 4.4).

FIG 4.3 The Material Selector Tool is grouped with the 3D Material Drop Tool.

FIG 4.4 3D Material Dropper Tool options bar showing the Materials library browser as well as the currently loaded material in the thumbnail (next to the Load Selected button in the options bar). You can also click this "Load Selected" button to load the currently selected material into the 3D Material Drop Tool.

## 4.2.2. Changing Material Color

It is very easy to change the color of your material and there are several ways to do it. The simplest way is to double-click the diffuse color and select a different color. If there is a texture associated with the diffuse map, you will see an icon like this: 🔖. If the Diffuse Map shows a texture associated with it and it doesn't contain any transparency, you will not see an effect if you simply change the diffuse by double-clicking on the color swatch. You will have to change the colors in the actual texture (image) or delete the texture and then double-click the diffuse swatch. You can open up this texture via the little popup of this same icon (Figure 4.5); choose "Open Texture" or you can double-click the texture from the texture list in the Layers panel. If you fill

FIG 4.5 Popup menu creating, loading, opening, editing or removing textures associated with materials.

this texture with a different color and hit "Save," and then "Close this .psb file," you will then see the color update on the material (similar to how Smart Objects work in Photoshop).

# 4.3. Painting on 3D

One of the great benefits of having 3D support in Photoshop is the ability to paint directly on models with all the amazing painting tools. There are seven different materials that can be painted on including Diffuse, Bump, Glossiness, Opacity, Shininess, Self-Illumination and Reflectivity. For greater detail on what these maps mean, refer to Chapter 1: Section 1.5. The most common maps to paint on are diffuse maps, opacity maps and bump maps. To target the particular map, choose the right map from the "Paint On" menu in the 3D Scene panel or from "3D Paint Mode" in the 3D menu (Figure 4.6).

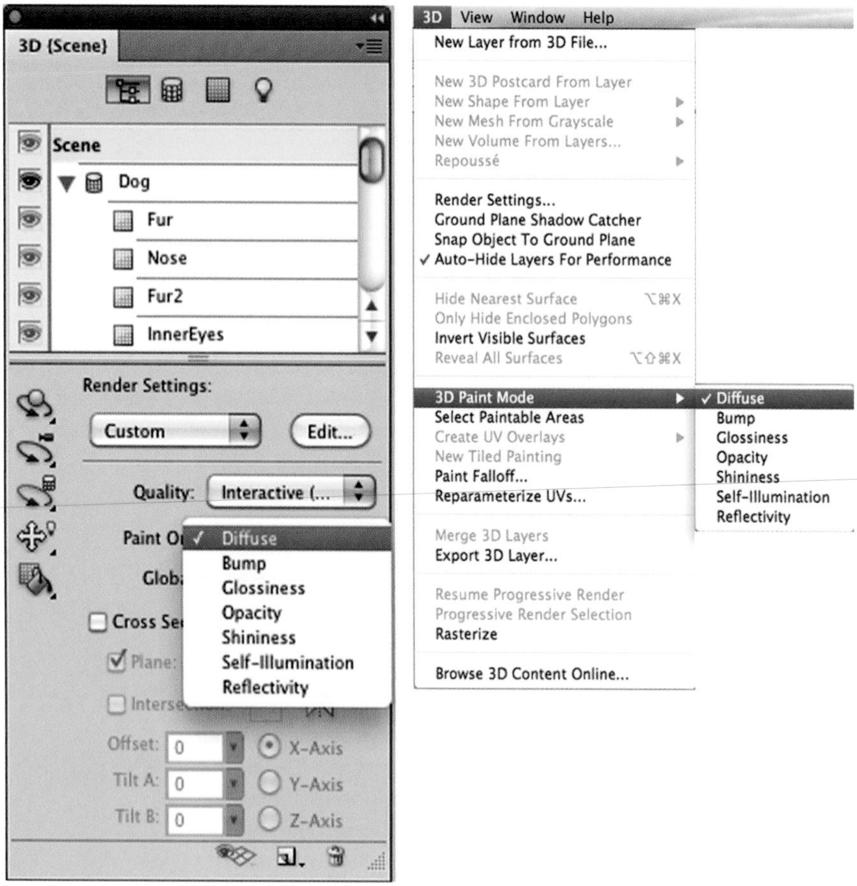

FIG 4.6 3D Scene panel paint on map selectors.

Photoshop 3D painting uses a projection-based model. This means that your 3D object has to be positioned in view so that paint can be properly applied. How the paint gets applied depends on the position of the object as well as scale. There are many tools in Photoshop that help with painting in 3D.

**Note:** It is recommended for faster performance to paint in the Interactive (Painting) or OpenGL mode.

### 4.3.1. Optimal Positioning of your 3D Model for Painting

To give a quick selection of areas that are ideal to paint on with the current position of the 3D object, from the 3D menu, choose "Select Paintable Areas." This will give you a marquee selection around ideal painting targets. Further, if an area falls out of this selection, you can reposition the object and reselect the paintable areas until your target falls within the selection. The Paint Mask Render setting is another useful tool to help with optimal positioning of your 3D object while painting. This can be found in the 3D Scene panel under the Render Setting presets (Figure 4.7).

FIG 4.7 3D Scene Panel Render Settings presets. Paint Mask mode is important to show you which area of your model is ideal to paint on.

FIG 4.8 This is the paint mask for the 3D dog object we've been using. At this scale and position, it is best to paint on areas that have been mapped to white. You can tell that the red areas are not optimal for painting as they are either not scaled correctly or not positioned directly in front of the screen.

**41**

In this mode, you cannot paint, but you have a simple way of visualizing what areas are ideal to paint on with the current 3D position. Areas mapped as white are ideal to paint on, areas mapped as blue are less ideal, and areas mapped as red are not ideal to paint on (i.e., they may be too far off the edge or not scaled optimally) (Figure 4.8). You can rotate your object (or scale) until the areas you want to paint on are mapped as white.

You can set the minimum and the maximum angles at which the paint falls off the edges by using the Paint Falloff command in the 3D menu.

## 4.3.2. Painting on Unwrapped Textures

On a Photoshop 3D layer, you can paint directly on the 3D model, or open up any associated textures and paint in 2D space. To do so, unwrap the texture by double-clicking it in the Layers panel or by choosing Open Texture from the fly-out of the attached texture (found in the 3D Materials panel) (Figure 4.9).

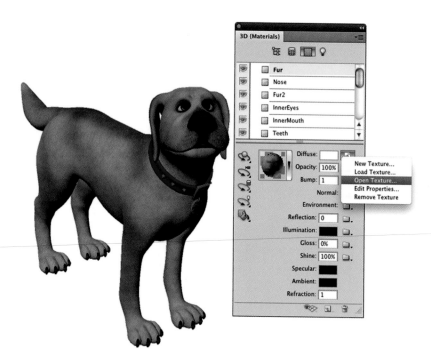

FIG 4.9 3D Materials panel and fly-out of a texture attached to the Diffuse Map.

With an unwrapped texture, you can view several overlays: Wireframe, Normal Map or Shaded under the 3D menu > Show Overlays. These are layers that get generated which serve as a guide when editing your unwrapped texture.

### 4.3.3. Reparameterizing UVs

In Section 1.6 in Chapter 1, we discussed UVs and UV Mapping. Choosing "Reparameterize UVs" uses Photoshop's built-in algorithm for assigning new UVs to your 3D model. It is important to note that this will mean that any textures currently applied to your model will no longer line up in the same place. Also, Photoshop's UV generation algorithm is optimized to create UVs that are good for painting on your 3D model; therefore, sometimes reparameterizing UVs can fix some unexpected painting behaviors. Unfortunately, due to the limitations of the algorithm this means that painting on your textures by opening them will be nearly impossible due to the texture fragments being broken up into many pieces; therefore, it is recommended that you paint directly on your 3D objects if you have reparameterized your UVs.

## 4.4. Tiled Painting

The Tiled Painting command takes the image and converts it into a tiled 3 × 3 grid. This is extremely useful in creating textures where you might want edits on edges to wrap around to the other side, or to remove seams to generate a larger patch of texture. Essentially, any edit you make will be repeated in the other tiles (Figure 4.10).

FIG 4.10 The far left image shows the original texture. After running the command to create new tiled painting, Photoshop will generate a 3 × 3 tiled grid (center) — original image shown here with a green boundary. The far right image shows a paint stroke (brown) on the edge gets repeated at all seams.

Photoshop essentially generates a 3D plane where the center image is the original texture. Because it's a 3D layer, you can add maps to create different effects. If you double-click on the diffuse map that was generated, you will have the image that you started with and all edits will be applied to this diffuse map. As a tiled painting, you have the flexibility of applying edits to a single tile and having it duplicate across the grid. Many painters use this feature so that they can have their paint strokes that fall off the edge wrap around to the other side.

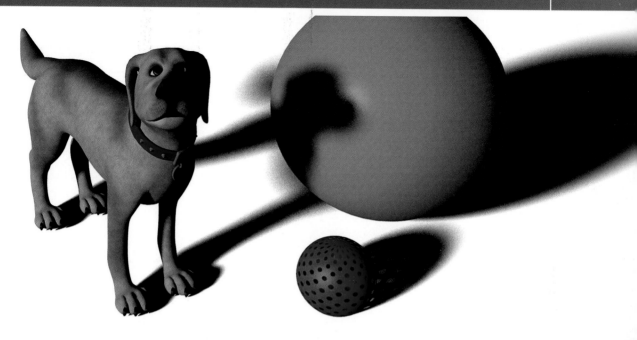

# CHAPTER 5

# Lights, Shadows and Final Rendering

## 5.1. Light Types

Photoshop ships with many light presets which you can use to light up your scene. From the 3D Lights panel, you can easily select a preset from the drop-down menu. You can also save light presets to be accessed here or in the Repoussé dialog (Figure 5.1). There are four types of lights you can add or edit in your scene. For a detailed description of these sources, check out Chapter 1: Section 1.4.

## 5.2. Positioning Lights and Keyboard Shortcuts

One way to position lights is to select a light and a light tool and use the 3D-Axis Widget to rotate, pan or slide. Point lights can only slide (you can't rotate a point light since it isn't a directional light). You can reposition your lights by using the on-canvas light widget (Figure 5.2). Check that you have 3D Ligts overlay on, a light selected in the 3D Scene Panel and a Light tool selected (Figure 5.3).

**FIG 5.1** Default Light presets found in the 3D Lights Panel. Select any preset to change the scene's lighting.

**3D in Photoshop. DOI: 10.1016/B978-0-240-81377-6.10005-5**

FIG 5.2 Upper-left corner shows the 3D Axis Tool for Lights (must have a light tool selected to see). If you turn on 3D Light overlay you can place your cursor over the widget (red by default) and reposition your light directly on-canvas.

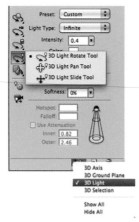

FIG 5.3 Turn the 3D Lights widgets on by showing Lights overlay from the bottom popup menu and select a light in the 3D Scene Panel.

Positioning a light can be difficult to get right. There are a couple of tools in Photoshop to help with this process. With any light tool selected, holding down the Option/Alt key and clicking on the canvas will target where that light should either point at (infinite and spot lights) or where the light should be moved to (point lights). You will see the cursor change to indicate a point target (similar to the cursor for defining a Clone Source with the Clone Stamp Tool).

Two more commands found in the 3D Lights panel can be very helpful. For spot lights, you can click on 🔧 which will point the light at the center of your scene. This is useful if you ended up getting your spot light point off in an undesirable direction and are having a hard time getting it pointed back at your scene. For all lights, you can click on 🔧 which will bring the light to where your current camera is (for light types that have a location) and point it in the direction of the camera (for light types that have a direction).

## 5.3. Editing Lights

Point, spot and infinite lights can be changed to most of the other light sources types; however, an image-based light cannot be changed to another light source. All light sources have a color and intensity applied and, further, they can have shadows generated from them. You can turn shadows on or off for individual lights as well as adjust the softness. The Shadow Opacity of a mesh determines how opaque the mesh is considered to be when casting a shadow. For some special effects, a shadow opacity of less than 100% might be useful where the shadow will exhibit the interior structure of the shadow caster. Typically though, the shadow opacity should be left at 100% and the Global Ambient Color is used to fill the shadowed regions with additional light. When an object should not cast a shadow at all, set the Shadow Opacity to 0. Brighter Global Ambient Colors produce lower contrast shadows. The Shadow Opacity field is found in the 3D Mesh Panel and the Global Ambient Color can be changed from the 3D Scene Panel.

## 5.4. Adding and Editing Shadows

Shadows are an important element in creating a realistic look or adding a creative effect to your design. How a shadow is generated is affected by many different elements in your scene. First and foremost, shadows require Ray Tracing in order to render. It is recommended that you edit your scene shadows using the Ray Trace (Draft) mode to quickly get a snapshot of how your shadow looks and where it's positioned. This setting can be found in the Quality drop-down of your 3D Scene Panel (Figure 5.4). Lights that cast on an object may generate a shadow onto other objects in the scene or the

FIG 5.4 The Quality menu with the option to choose "Ray Trace (Draft)" in the 3D Scene panel. This is important when editing and adding shadows.

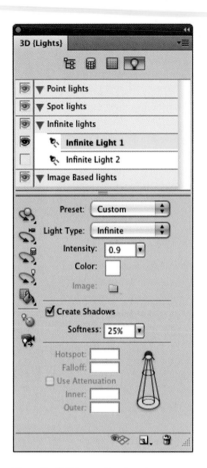

FIG 5.5 The 3D Lights panel has the option to create shadows and determine the softness of that shadow from each light source

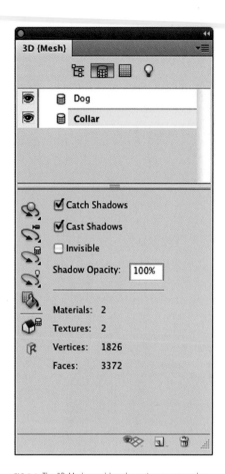

FIG 5.6 The 3D Mesh panel has the options to set meshes to catch and cast shadows as well as adjust Shadow Opacity.

ground. How these shadows look can be controlled with properties of the Light(s) or with properties of the mesh(es).

Lights can have the options to generate shadows and determine how soft the edges of these shadows get rendered (Figure 5.5). Meshes have the option to catch shadows as well as cast shadows (from the light source they intercept). Further, you can adjust how transparent these shadows are using the same panel (Figure 5.6).

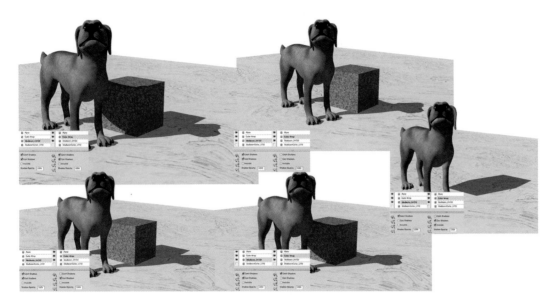

FIG 5.7 Different ways you can cast or catch shadows on different objects in the scene.

These controls will also affect the shadows that are created between meshes in the same scene. For example, you can have two meshes in a scene where one mesh will catch shadows and the other will cast shadows (Figure 5.7).

Further, you can target a mesh to be invisible but at the same time catch a shadow. This is important if, for example, you want a plane to catch a shadow of your object but you don't want the plane to be visible. This is also a very useful technique when trying to integrate 3D renderings into an existing photograph (see third image going clockwise from the top-left image in (Figure 5.7). Starting from the top-left image in Figure 5.7, both the dog as well as the cube are casting shadows onto the ground. Further, the cube is catching a shadow from the dog. In the next image to the right, the cube is not catching a shadow nor is it casting a shadow on the ground. The only shadow visible on the ground is the one that the dog is casting. The next image on the far right is where the cube is set as an invisible mesh casting a shadow. The shadow from the dog is not set to cast onto the ground. The bottom center image shows the dog casting a shadow and the cube catching the shadow of the dog but it itself is not casting a shadow. Finally, we have the bottom-left image where the dog and the cube are casting shadows but the cube is not catching a shadow from the dog.

**FIG 5.8** Shadow cast on the ground plane of the scene. This functions as an invisible shadow catcher (plane) for your object.

## 5.4.1. Ground Shadows and Snapping Object to Ground Plane

Ground shadows can be created by turning on the option in the 3D menu or in the fly-out of the 3D Scene panel. This option will generate shadows on the ground plane of your scene where the plane is always "invisible." This serves as an invisible shadow catcher for your 3D layer (Figure 5.8).

Often your object may be too far from your ground plane for the ground plane to catch the shadow. If this occurs, you can use the "Snap the Object to Ground Plane" command from the 3D menu, which will snap the closest point of your 3D object to the ground plane.

**Note**: Remember that in order to see shadows you have to be in Ray Trace Draft or Final mode.

## 5.5. Colored Transparent Shadows

In the image below, we have a scene with a plane on the ground which will catch the shadows, an opaque window frame, an opaque glass object and a point light placed behind the window (indicated by the white Light overlay widget). The shadow that is cast in this configuration is a completely black shadow:

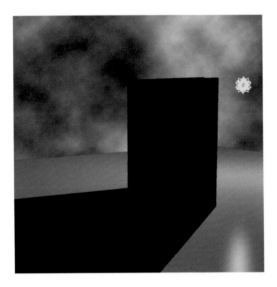

If we set the window's Opacity to 50%, we get the following image:

As you can see, a semi-transparent shadow is cast and the window is semi-transparent. Now let's try to get some color in that shadow. If we set the diffuse color of the glass object to red (255, 0, 0). We get the following image:

Note that the shadow on the ground is tinted red. But why isn't the glass itself red? This is because the light is behind the glass pane so when the Ray Tracer does its lighting calculation, it gets back black. In this particular scenario if we want the glass pane to also be red, we must set it to red using the self-illumination parameter. Setting the Self-Illumination to red we get the following image:

Although this seems like a lot of steps to get the desired result, it does allow the user a great level of flexibility by being able to control the color of the shadow vs. the color of the transmitted light separately.

Now let's consider a different scenario in which the light is moved in front of the window pane. Now you can set the Self-Illumination back to 0 and, with the same Opacity of 50% from before, we get the expected behavior — a red shadow with a red pane:

When the light is positioned in front of the object, both the object and the shadow accurately respond to the properties of the light and reflect the red color. When the light was positioned behind the object, because Photoshop does not support double-sided lighting, the object did not respond to the reflection of the light and therefore, the effect was mimicked using self-illumination.

Now let's set the Opacity of the window to be 10%:

The window becomes more transparent and the redness in the shadow is reduced. Now let's set the Opacity to 85%:

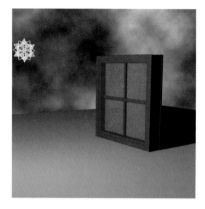

The window becomes brighter red and the shadow gets darker. So, how do I get a bright red (255, 0, 0) shadow? Unfortunately, this is not going to be possible in the current version of Photoshop. With a 50% Opacity you will get a shadow that is 50% the diffuse color of the object casting the shadow. As the opacity increases, the shadow will get darker. As the opacity decreases the shadow will get lighter. However, the color of the shadow will never be the same color as the object that is casting the shadow.

One potential work-around in the case where the glass object is back-lit as it was originally would be to create a 32-bit diffuse texture and set the color brighter (i.e., 2.0, 0, 0 for red instead of 1, 0, 0). However, this work-around will not work if the object is front-lit. Another work-around is to increase the intensity of the lights. This has the side effect that the entire scene's illumination is also increased — which may be undesirable.

It is also possible to do stained glass effects by using the same texture for the self-illumination map as the diffuse map:

**Tip: Shadows During Interaction**. It can often be very useful to see your shadows change as you interact with your scene. This can be achieved using the Adobe Ray Tracer (Draft or Final), which must be turned on using the settings in the 3D Preferences panel. See Chapter 2 Ray Tracing and the section before this (5.4 Adding and Editing Shadows) for more information on how to do this.

## 5.6. Final Rendering

Rendering your final scene is an important step in the 3D design process — as it is the only way you can see many of the advanced effects Photoshop has to offer. Photoshop has a Ray Tracer that renders all the final lighting, shadows, reflections and refractions. For more detailed information on the Ray Tracer, see Chapter 2.

Rendering with the Ray Tracer can be set from the 3D Scene panel under the Quality menu. There are two modes of Ray Trace rendering — Draft and Final. Draft will be quicker than Final and will give you a general idea of how your final lighting will look. The amount of time it takes for final rendering to be complete is dependent on many factors including the resolution of the document, how complex your scene is and what quality maximum is set from the 3D section in Preferences (Figure 5.9).

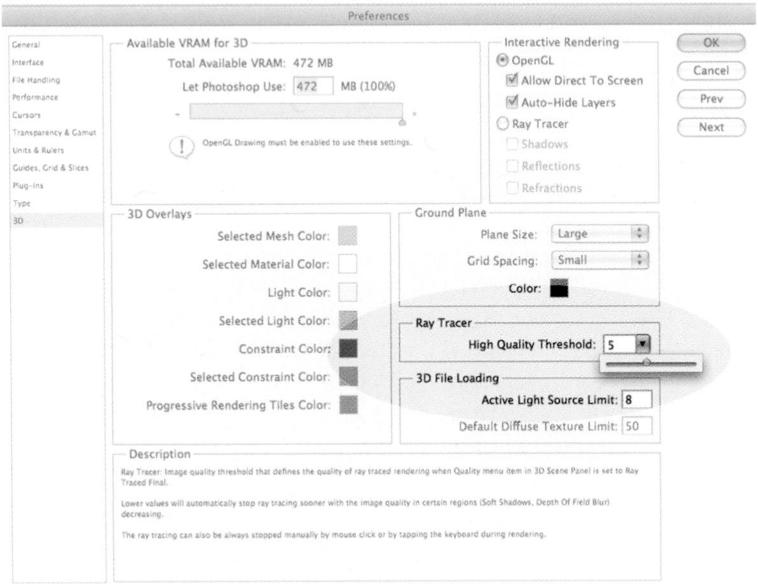

**FIG 5.9** Go to the 3D section in Preferences to set "High Quality Threshold" for Final Ray Tracing.

In Photoshop CS5 Extended, *progressive rendering* was added for the Adobe Ray Tracer. This means that your scene will be rendered progressively, or in stages (a certain number of passes), allowing you to quickly get an initial feel of what your lighting will look like as an indication that rendering is incomplete. At any stage of rendering, Photoshop will draw a grid overlaying the area that is currently being rendered. When rendering is complete, the grid (tiles) are no longer drawn (Figure 5.10).

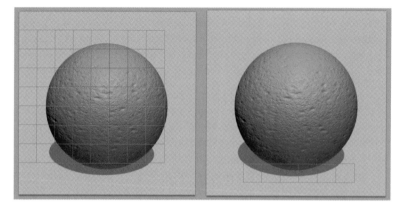

FIG 5.10 Blue grid overlay showing you areas in the scene that are getting rendered. In the image on the right, most of the orange itself is fully rendered (no grid drawn) whereas the shadow (grid overlay drawn) is still rendering.

You can pause your render at any time by clicking the mouse or by pressing the spacebar or Esc key. To resume the render, choose 3D > Resume Progressive Render from the 3D menu or from the 3D flyout in the panel.

## 5.6.1. Test Rendering

Photoshop can test render any selection easily. This means that you can take any part of your 3D scene and only render that section. For instance, it is useful to run a test rendering on shadows if you have a particularly complex lighting setup where you may want to see how shadows are rendering. Simply make a selection around the area you want to be rendered and run the command "3D > Progressive Render Selection". This is important if you don't want to wait for the whole scene to render before knowing what a certain part of your scene will look like.

# CHAPTER 6

# REPOUSSÉ

## Adobe Repoussé — 3D Extrusions

## 6.1. Introduction to Adobe Repoussé

Adobe Repoussé is a feature that allows you to produce a 3D shape from closed paths. It is named after the metalworking technique of shaping a metal by hammering a pattern from the reverse side.

The Adobe Repoussé feature can be invoked from the 3D panel in Photoshop or from the 3D menu.

Adobe Repoussé relies on OpenGL Drawing. This means that you must have a GPU (video card) that is compatible with Photoshop CS5 Extended. If your video card doesn't support OGL Drawing in Photoshop, the Repoussé menu item in the 3D menu will be grayed out and Repoussé will not work. For more information on OpenGL, see Chapter 2: Section 2.1.

Repoussé can be invoked on one of four types of objects: text layer, layer mask, selection or path (Figure 6.1). Repoussé converts the paths from each of the input types into an editable collection of surfaces called a Repoussé

**3D in Photoshop. DOI: 10.1016/B978-0-240-81377-6.10006-7**

FIG 6.1 Repoussé can be invoked from the 3D panel or from the 3D menu.

patch. The area bounded by the input path forms the front of the Repoussé patch. The front is surrounded by the front bevel surface. The Repoussé patch also has a back and back bevel surface opposite the front and front bevel surface respectively. Finally, the extrusion connecting the front bevel to the back bevel is the side surface (Figure 6.2).

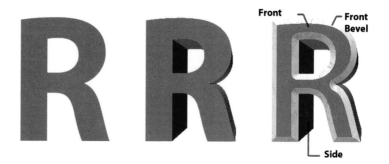

FIG 6.2 Starting with the letter R, Adobe Repoussé is used to extrude it to a 3D text object. The Repoussé object consists of a front and back surface, a front and back bevel and a side extrusion.

In the Repoussé dialog, you can independently change the shape of all five surfaces of the Repoussé patch. Similarly, you can independently set material properties for all five surfaces of the Repoussé patch. Any of the changes made in the Repoussé panel will be immediately previewed on the document canvas. The Repoussé patch can be transformed directly on the Photoshop canvas by the usual mesh transformation tools or the 3D-Axis Widget (Figure 6.3). Hitting Cancel in the Repoussé panel will undo these changes and close the Repoussé panel.

The main controls for the Repoussé object are found in the Repoussé dialog (see Figure 6.4).

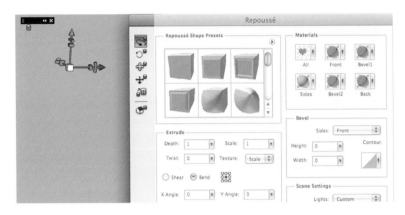

**FIG 6.3** Use the Mesh rotation tools located on the side of the Repoussé dialog or use the 3D Axis Tool on canvas to reposition your object.

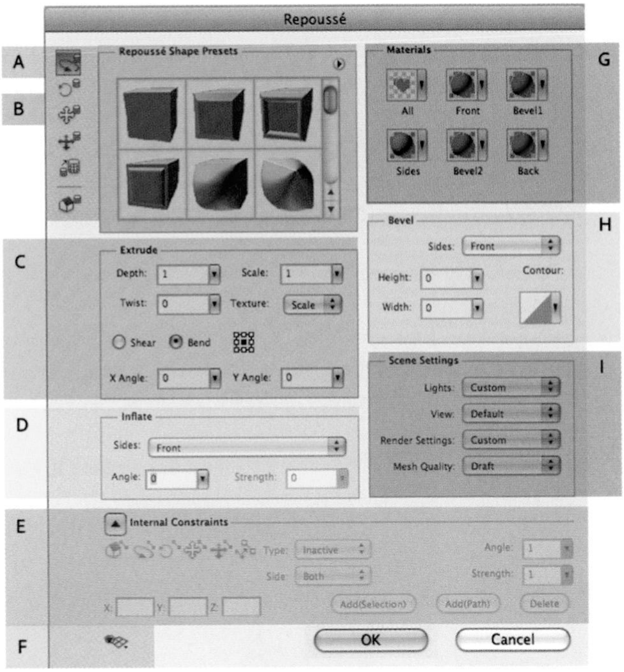

**FIG 6.4 The Repoussé dialog**

A — 3D Mesh controls to rotate, roll, pan, slide, scale and to revert to default position. B — Shape presets to change geometry. C — Extrude parameters. D — Inflate parameters that can be applied to Front and/or Back faces. E — Constraint controls to set parameters for internal subpaths (or selections). F — View 3D overlays including 3D-Axis Tool, Mesh boundaries, Lights and Ground Plane. G — Material libraries and picker for the different Repoussé surfaces. H — Bevel parameters that can be applied to Front and/or back faces. I — Scene Settings where you can select Light presets, Saved Mesh positions, Render Settings and Mesh Quality.

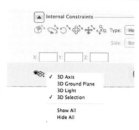

FIG 6.5 The 3D Overlay toggles found in the Repoussé dialog are also found in the 3D Scene panel.

There are three properties you can change using the Repoussé dialog: Shape, Materials and Rendering. Of these, the Shape changes are the only ones unique to the Repoussé dialog; you can change Material, Positioning, Lighting and Rendering properties from the 3D panel (Window > 3D) outside the Repoussé dialog as well.

Many of the scene navigation tools from the 3D panel are also provided in the Repoussé dialog for your convenience. As shown in Figure 6.4, you can cycle through Light presets, observe the Repoussé patch from different viewpoints and change the Render settings. In addition, in the bottom left of the dialog, you'll see toggle switches for displaying the 3D Mesh overlays, Ground Plane, Lights and the 3D-Axis Widget. This is the same Overlay menu you get in the 3D panel (Figure 6.5).

## 6.2. Changing the Repoussé Shape

### 6.2.1. Presets

The quickest way to significantly alter the default 3D shape is to choose one of the Repoussé presets from the top-left section of the Repoussé panel. These presets are pre-determined combinations of extrusion, bevel and inflation parameters (which are described below). After selecting a preset, it can be further fine-tuned by changing individual parameters. Additionally, you can save your preferred combination of individual Repoussé parameters as a custom preset from the fly-out menu in the Repoussé presets section.

**Extrusion, Depth, Twist, and Scale**

The extrusion (side) surface can be made longer by changing the Depth slider. This parameter controls the amount of extrusion and is commonly found in other 3D modeling applications. The extrusion can also be twisted by changing the twist angle. The twist angle specifies the total twist between the front and the back surfaces and is distributed evenly along the extrusion surface. Finally, the extrusion can be scaled so the back surface is a scaled

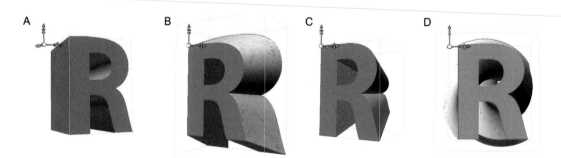

FIG 6.6 A — Simple extrusion applied to the letter R. B — Scale applied where the back face is scaled larger than the front face. C — Scale applied where the back face is scaled smaller than the front face. D — Simple twist applied to the letter R.

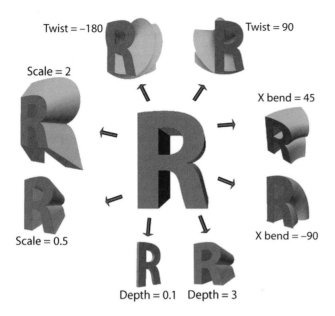

Twist = −180    Twist = 90

Scale = 2

X bend = 45

Scale = 0.5    X bend = −90

Depth = 0.1    Depth = 3

**FIG 6.7** Variety of different extrusion parameters applied.

version of the front surface, with the extrusion surface smoothly growing or shrinking to connect the front to the back (Figures 6.6 and 6.7).

## Bend and Shear

In Repoussé, you can create curved extrusions by applying a bend to the extrusion as well as a shear effect (where the front and back surfaces move parallel to each other). To simulate a lathe using Repoussé (Figure 6.8), pick an X bend angle of 360 degrees and change the reference point to lie on the right edge of the bounding box (any one of the three points). To lathe in the opposite direction, pick an X bend angle of −360 degrees and pick the

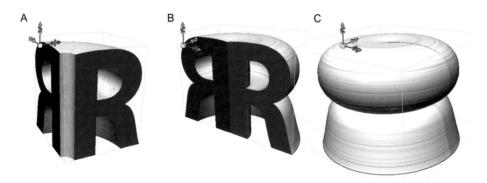

A    B    C

**FIG 6.8** A — A simple bend to the left applied with an extrusion depth of 1. B — A simple bend to the left applied with a 0 extrusion depth and a reference point set to be the center left. C — A 360 degree bend applied to the letter R. This simulates what is commonly referred to as a *lathe*.

reference point to lie on the left edge of the bounding box. For a smooth curve, make sure that you have your Mesh Quality set to high for more information on this, refer to Section 6.5 in this Chapter.

A powerful method for generating a vast variety of shapes is to change the reference point for all of the above extrusion parameters. The reference point ⊞ is a temporary 'origin' point used by the extrusion twist, scale and bend operations to measure distances. By default, the reference point is the center of the 2D bounding box of the input path. However, you can change the reference point to be on the edge of the bounding box, or even on one of the corners. Changing the reference point changes the way in which the twist, scale and bend extrusion parameters control the shape, so you can produce drastically different shapes by simply changing the reference point.

## Bevel

Beveling allows you to simulate a process that cuts away the boundary edges that the Repoussé shape forms along the boundaries of the front and back surfaces. To expose the bevel surfaces, move the Width and Height sliders — the height can be positive (where the front or back surface is pushed out) or negative (where the front or back surface is pushed in). The bevel surface is hidden when its width is zero. By default, the beveled edge is a straight line (Linear preset) and flat. However, it can be set to any preset contour shapes (Figure 6.9 and 6.10).

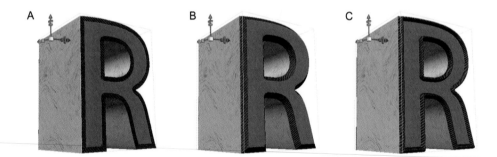

FIG 6.9  A — Default settings with no bevel applied (0 height and width). B — Simple Linear preset bevel applied. C — Simple Cone preset applied.

Clicking on the contour thumbnail ◢ will bring up a bevel profile editor that allows you to construct custom contours in the same way that you would in the Bevel and Emboss section of the Layer Effects dialog. The bevel mesh will update interactively as you change the bevel profile contour.

## Inflation

A unique ability in Repoussé is to smoothly inflate or "puff out" the front or back surfaces. Inflating the surface gives a unique 3D look to the originally flat surface (Figure 6.11).

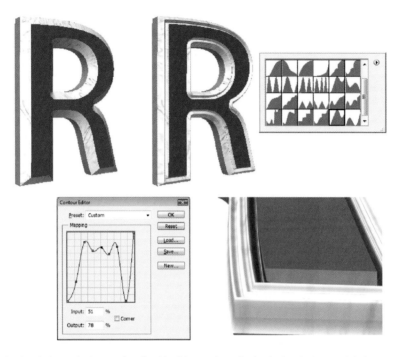

**FIG 6.10** Custom bevel applied using the Contour editor (found by clicking on the profile thumbnail in the Repoussé dialog).

**FIG 6.11** Smooth inflation applied to the front of this letter R.

The front or back surface is inflated by changing the angle it makes at the boundary. Additionally, you can change the strength with which the angle condition must be maintained. A high strength value will propagate the angle requirement further from the boundary; zero angle and strength will have the default flat behavior.

Note that inflation can be performed only on the front and back surfaces, and the bevel and extrusion surfaces are unchanged during the inflation parameter changes.

## 6.3. Constraints

Constraints are internal paths fully contained within closed paths. If you take a look at the example we've been using with the letter R, there is an internal constraint identified as the hole in this letter. Note that fonts are treated specially in Repoussé where the holes are automatically identified. However, for all other paths or selections, you have the option to select the constraint to be a hole or to be filled (Figure 6.12). For more information on creating holes with Repoussé see below.

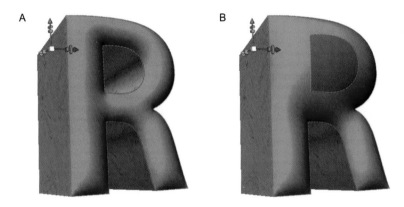

FIG 6.12 A — For text, by default Photoshop will define constraints (blue dotted line) to be a hole. B — This same constraint can be changed to a filled constraint ('active') where separate extrusion parameters can be applied relative to the bounding path or selection.

These internal paths may exist in the input paths originally provided to Repoussé, or additional constraints may be added at any time to the front Repoussé patch. To add constraints to an existing Repoussé patch, the user first draws paths or selections from outside the Repoussé panel. After drawing the paths or selections, add them as constraints from the Repoussé sub-menu of the 3D menu or from the Internal Constraints drop-down section of the Repoussé panel (Figures 6.13). Only paths that are fully contained within the front surface and do not intersect existing constraints or boundaries can be added as new constraints.

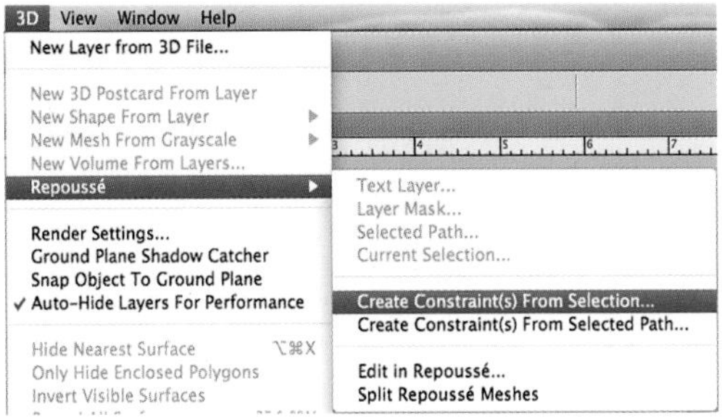

**FIG 6.13** Constraints can be added to existing Repoussé patches in the 3D menu as well as by using the Constraints controls in the Repoussé dialog (see Figure 6.14).

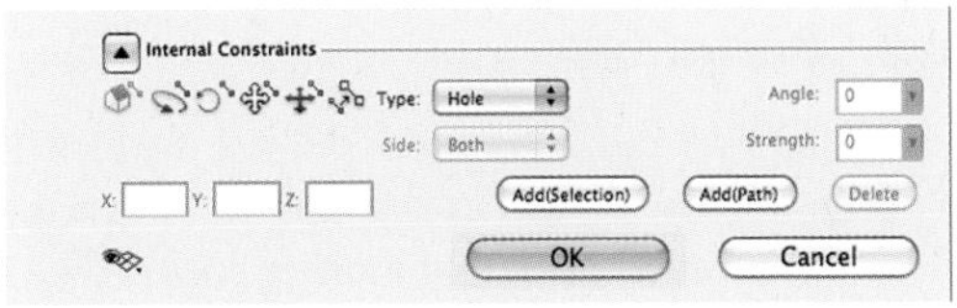

**FIG 6.14** Constraints can be added using the Internal Constraints controls found at the bottom of the Repoussé dialog and hitting the Add (Selection) and Add (Path) buttons.

Constraints are used as handles for modifying the front surface of the Repoussé patch. The constraints can be manipulated directly by the constraint tools. The rest of the surface will smoothly deform to pass through the constraints. The shape of the surface near constraints can further be modified by using the angle and strength parameters and behave similar to the parameters used to inflate the surface.

## 6.3.1. Holes

The most common type of constraint is the "hole" constraint. Fonts are treated specially in Repoussé where the holes are automatically identified. For example, with the letter "R" the inside of the R is automatically detected as a hole and will be "punched-out". Whenever a hole is added to the front surface, one automatically is added to the back. Therefore, you will be able to see through both the front and the back face to the background. Similarly, when you change the position of the hole on the front, a similar change will happen to the hole on the back. Since the hole is on the boundary of the surface, when you change the patch-wide inflation parameters, the surface will be inflated near the hole as well. The hole can be converted into an active constraint or an inactive constraint (Figure 6.15). For a constraint to be made into or added as a hole, it must be a closed path.

FIG 6.15 The same letter "R" where the constraint in the middle is set as a "hole" and manipulated independently from the existing bounding shape/path using the constraint rotation tools found at the bottom of the Repoussé dialog (see Figure 6.4).

## 6.3.2. Active Constraints

Active constraints affect the surface on both sides of the path. Like holes, active constraints can be moved, and the surface near the active constraint can be further inflated using the angle and strength parameters. The inflation parameters can be independently varied on either side of the constraint. Unlike holes, active constraint when added to the front, are not added to the back surface. Also unlike holes, active constraints can be open or closed paths (Figure 6.16).

FIG 6.16 **Distorting Photographs with Active Constraints**
First, we convert this photograph to a 3D plane by selecting the whole image and creating a Repoussé patch. We then draw a polygon around the subject, add it as an active constraint and move it up. The pixels inside the constraint are undistorted, and the pixels outside the constraint stretch to satisfy the new constraint position.

## 6.3.3. Inactive Constraints

Inactive constraints are placeholder constraints that have been "turned off." They are useful in cases where you may have too many internal constraints, and want to use only some of them. This may happen if you have a complicated path with many internal sub-paths and you may not want to individually manipulate all of them — some of the paths might remain "inactive" or without any extrusion properties added. The inactive constraints lie on the surface and are only modified by neighboring surface changes. However, they do not affect the surface. Automatically making all sub-paths active can cause performance degradation; therefore, Photoshop automatically leaves sub-paths inactive until user changes it. Inactive constraints can be changed to the active or hole type constraints at any time: the constraint position will be set to its initial position and will need to be transformed using the constraint tools to match their desired positions.

## 6.4. Assigning Materials

In addition to changing the shape of the Repoussé patch, you can also change the material of any of the five patch surfaces. The material picker in the top-right section of the Repoussé panel is used for high-level material specification. The material of any of the five surfaces can be specified by clicking the drop-down thumbnail icon for the corresponding surface. The same material can be applied to all five surfaces by clicking the thumbnail labeled "All."

### 6.4.1. Extrusion Texture Mapping

As described earlier, materials often contain texture maps that control the appearance of the shape. The extrusion (side) surface has three options for specifying the texture mapping method. These three options are "Scale," "Tile" and "Fill." These options are found in the drop-down box labeled "Texture" in the Extrude section of the Repoussé dialog (see Figure 6.4).

**Scale**
The Scale option scales the texture to exactly fit the extrusion, such that one side of the texture map completely goes around the boundary, and the other side of the texture map spans the entire depth of the extrusion.

**Tile**
The Tile option will assign the texture map without any scaling, and will tile the texture if the extrusion surface area is greater than the texture area.

**Fill**
The Fill option will scale the texture such that the smaller dimension of the texture map will exactly fit the larger dimension of the extrusion surface (either perimeter of boundary or extrusion depth).

## 6.5. Mesh Quality

Some patches with highly curved extrusions, complicated bevel profiles, large inflation angles or transformed constraints may look tessellated or "blocky." Improving the mesh quality will reduce these tessellation artifacts. In the Scene Settings section (see Figure 6.4) of the Repoussé dialog, you'll see a Mesh Quality drop-down menu. Improving the mesh quality will produce denser meshes with smaller triangles for all five Repoussé surfaces. Since increasing the mesh quality produces denser meshes, you will notice a slowdown in rendering and Repoussé parameter updates. You should not set the quality to High until you are done editing the shape of your object.

### 6.5.1. Repoussé Speed

The speed with which Repoussé interacts to user input depends strongly on the number of samples (points) of the input paths. A larger path will have more samples. Similarly, a densely sampled path will have more samples. For example, Repoussé will be much slower on a path drawn on a 300 ppi document than for the same path drawn on a 72 ppi document. For large documents, you can invoke Repoussé on a smaller path (to have faster interaction speeds) and use the mesh scaling tools to expand the Repoussé patch after exiting the Repoussé dialog.

## 6.6. Split Apart Functionality

You may invoke Repoussé on a string of text (or a number of disjoint paths) and Photoshop will still produce a single Repoussé patch (or mesh). If you want to break apart the different pieces of the patch into separate Repoussé patches (or meshes), you can use the "Split Apart" functionality found in the 3D menu under Repoussé (Figures 6.17 and 6.18).

Alternatively, to achieve the same result you can start with separate meshes or 3D layers initially and then later merge the object together. You will see more on this later in Chapter 9.

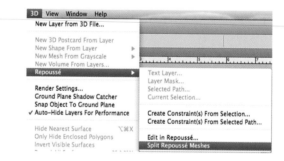

FIG 6.17 The Split Repoussé Meshes command is useful if you would like to generate separate meshes for each letter in a string of text or to separate disjointed objects where a single Repoussé object was created. Having separate meshes will enable you to position the different letters (or objects) independently and enable you to assign different materials to each object.

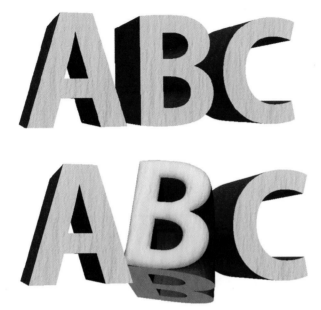

FIG 6.18 String of text "ABC" where the single text layer was first created as a single Repoussé patch (top) and then split apart (bottom) to independently manipulate the letter "B" from the others.

# CHAPTER 7

# Performance Settings and Optimization

## 7.1. 3D Preferences

The 3D preferences can be found in a Preference panel in the Preferences dialog. It can be accessed by opening any Preference panel and selecting 3D on the tab selector to the right, or it can be opened directly using Preferences > 3D menu item. Since many of the features in Photoshop 3D depend on OpenGL, the GPU Memory, Interactive Rendering, 3D Overlays and Ground Plane controls are only enabled when OpenGL is available and turned on in the Performance preference tab (Figure 7.1).

**Note**: In order for Photoshop to communicate with your graphics card to achieve accelerated 3D rendering, it must do so through a piece of software called the graphics driver. This driver is usually provided by the manufacturer of your video card but in some cases, such as certain laptops, it will be provided by the laptop manufacturer. In order to assure that your 3D functionality works properly, it is important that you have the most up-to-date

**3D in Photoshop. DOI: 10.1016/B978-0-240-81377-6.10007-9**

**FIG 7.1** 3D Preferences found in Photoshop Preferences dialog.

graphics drivers for your hardware. For more information on graphics car see Chapter 2, Section 2.1.

## 7.2. GPU Memory (VRAM)

**FIG 7.2** Preferences to set general Memory Usage in Photoshop.

In the upper-left corner of the 3D Preferences, you can change the total amount of VRAM available for 3D features in Photoshop. VRAM is used by your GPU card and is separate from your system memory (RAM). Settings for general memory allocation are found in the Performance section Photoshop Preferences (Figure 7.2). Video memory is also used by other (non-3D) features within Photoshop that are dependent on OGL (i.e. Canvas Rotation), other applications dependent on OGL as well as the operating system; therefore, the VRAM setting in the 3D section of your Photoshop Preferences only allocates a portion of the total VRAM available while saving a certain (non-editable) amount of VRAM for capabilities outside of 3D in Photoshop. In other words, the operating system and other parts of Photoshop are using some of the installed VRAM, so the available amount is going to be less than the total amount that your GPU has. For most users, the default value set will be appropriate. However, there are two cases in which change is necessary:

- Case 1: One or more GPU-dependent programs are running in parallel with Adobe Photoshop, such as Adobe Premiere or a 3D modeling tool. If you would like for them to have more GPU memory available, you should reduce Photoshop's VRAM allotment.
- Case 2: Your 3D workflow involves a 3D model with many triangles and/or large textures and no other GPU-dependent programs are running. To ensure maximum performance, set the VRAM limit closer to its maximum.

# 7.3. Interactive Rendering

Interacting rendering is the rendering that occurs during operations where the mouse button is down in the upper right corner of the 3D preferences. The controls in the 3D preferences (shown in Figure 7.1) allow you to tune the interactive rendering experience. The default state of these controls allows for maximum performance during interaction, and in this section we describe the ways (and reasons) to change it.

## 7.3.1. OpenGL (on by default)

In this mode, during interaction, rendering always switches to OpenGL mode, even if rendering quality in the 3D panel is set to one of the Ray Trace options. This allows for better performance, but will turn off Ray Tracer-only effects, such as shadows.

## 7.3.2. Allow Direct To Screen (on by default)

With this on, OpenGL rendering will bypass the Photoshop layer blending mechanism, and render the result directly to screen during interaction. This setting allows for maximum possible speed and fully uses GPU acceleration.

## 7.3.3. Auto-Hide Layers (on by default)

If enabled, all other layers and the current 3D layer's Layer Effects are turned off during interaction and the final composite is only displayed on mouse-up. If disabled, Photoshop blending is active during interaction and while 3D rendering is still performed with OpenGL, compositing overhead may result in a noticeable performance decrease Auto-Hide Layers for Performance can also be turned on and off from the 3D menu in Photoshop (Figure 7.3).

**FIG 7.3** Auto-Hide Layers can be turned on from the 3D menu to maximize performance and GPU acceleration.

## 7.3.4. Ray Tracer (off by default)

This setting forces ray tracing during interaction, which will result in a significant performance reduction depending on the number and speed of your computer's cores. Shadows, Reflection and Refraction are effects that can be individually turned on or off when choosing the Ray Tracer for interaction. Each effect will cumulatively slowdown performance so it is not recommended that you have all effects on when using the Ray Tracer for interaction. The option to use the Ray Tracer during interaction showing just Shadows, can be particularly useful when trying to get shadows to appear in the right place but are generally slow to render.

# 7.4. Ray Trace Quality Threshold

Image quality threshold is specified as a number between 1 and 10. This number defines the quality of a Ray Traced rendering when the Quality menu item in the 3D Scene panel is set to Ray Traced Final (Figure 7.4). Lower threshold values will stop the rendering sooner as a result of fewer passes with the Ray Tracer. This has a direct affect on the quality of Ray Tracing effects such as soft shadows or depth of field. In general, if your image remains noisy after completing a Final Render, you may want to increase the threshold to allow for more passes of rendering your scene.

## 7.5. 3D File Loading

These settings allow you to impose limits during loading of 3D files. Since imported 3D files can potentially have a lot of light sources and materials, loading and initial rendering of these scenes can take a very long time, and, depending on your workflow, might be unnecessary.

### 7.5.1. Active Light Source Limit

Active Light Source Limit sets the limit for active lights. If the number of light sources in the incoming 3D file exceeds the limit, some light sources will be initially turned off. Note that you can still turn them on using the eye icon next to the light source object in a Scene view or Lights view (Figure 7.5).

**FIG 7.4** Ray Trace Quality setting in the 3D Panel where quality is dependent on the threshold determined in 3D Preferences.

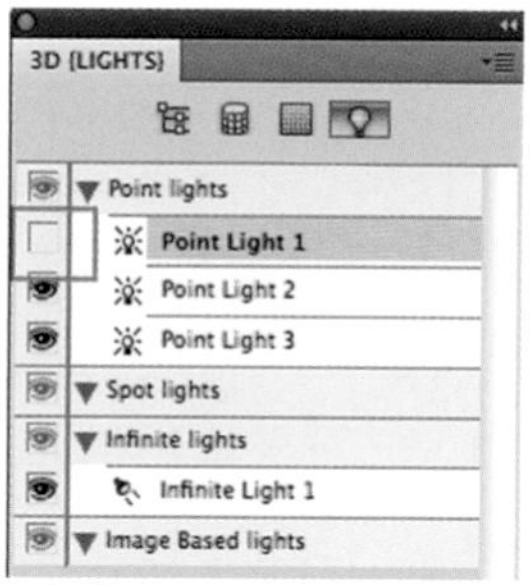

**FIG 7.5** The eye icon in the 3D Lights Panel allow you to toggle lights on and off.

# PART III

# Workflows

## In this part

Now that you have both an understanding of basic 3D concepts as well as an introduction to how 3D works in Photoshop, you can start having some real fun in this section. In Part III, we have several amazing artists that will walk you through useful and fun techniques using 3D in Photoshop. For both those new to 3D as well as the seasoned 3D user, you'll find great tips and tricks on how to composite, create 3D objects, add effects, create lenticulars and how to work with lighting, cameras, shadows and many more. Each artist has different workflows that will give you a taste of what can be accomplished using all the great new 3D tools.

# CHAPTER 8

# 3D and Compositing with Bert Monroy

With the introduction of 3D in Photoshop, I have been very curious as to how this affected the average Photoshop user. I have found that many are extremely curious as to what it is all about but doubt that it will be part of their daily workflow. However, 3D has made its way into just about every aspect of the graphic arts world. What started out as a gimmick to get people into theaters back in the 1950s has evolved to become an integral part of TV commercials, magazine ads and, of course, movies. We are now being bombarded with advertising for 3D televisions! 3D has become the big kid on the block.

The commercials and ads mentioned earlier are not the "pop off the screen" effects that we get in movies, but rather the simple depiction of a product or scene. Car commercials are a great example of this use of 3D. There is a TV commercial where hundreds of automobiles are driving around forming giant patterns and pictures to illustrate the narrator's comments. Think of the logistical nightmare of having all those drivers synchronized to do the job that is so easily accomplished with 3D models instead.

3D in Photoshop. DOI: 10.1016/B978-0-240-81377-6.10008-0

**FIG 8.1** Close up of MTV storefront from the painting "Times Square".

"I will never have to create or use a 3D automobile," you are probably thinking right now. "I have no need for 3D objects at all" might be crossing your thoughts as well. I want to share with you some places where the introduction of a simple 3D effect has made things so much easier in my workflow.

In the creation of my latest painting there were two places where 3D simplified an effect that used to require a lot of effort to create. I want to share one of those instances with you here in this chapter.

Figure 8.1 shows the top frame of a storefront on New York's Times Square. Notice the vertical blinds that run across the façade. To accomplish this in the past, I resorted to Adobe Illustrator where I would create a single vertical line of a thick weight for the blind closest to the viewer. I would then create a second, thinner line for the blind furthest away. Using the Blend Tool in Illustrator a blend was generated between the two lines giving the result of the lines getting thinner as they moved away from the viewer. This was not enough. The blend sets the additional lines equidistant from each other — that is not the way it would look in real life. The lines would get thinner and also appear to get closer together. To accomplish the latter, I would then have to "expand" the blend then physically select each line and move it into place. This was done by eye — constantly adjusting the lines until they looked correct. That many steps were painstaking to say the least.

The 3D feature in Photoshop has turned this into a simple process that almost requires no thought. A single line is turned into a pattern and a layer is filled with that pattern (Figure 8.2).

That layer is converted into a 3D postcard (3D > New 3D Postcard From Layer). The postcard is then moved into 3D space, accomplishing the desired effect as seen in Figure 8.3.

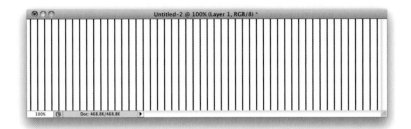

FIG 8.2 Layer filled with a pattern of vertical lines.

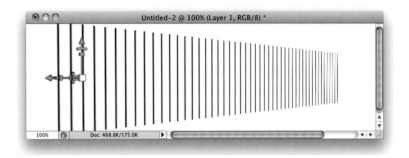

FIG 8.3 3D Postcard layer angled into perspective.

Since the content of the layer is being manipulated in actual three-dimensional space, the lines get thinner and closer together as they travel away from the point of view. Figure 8.4 shows the 3D postcard of the lines in position over the window areas in the scene.

FIG 8.4 Lines in place prior to being clipped with the layer containing the windows.

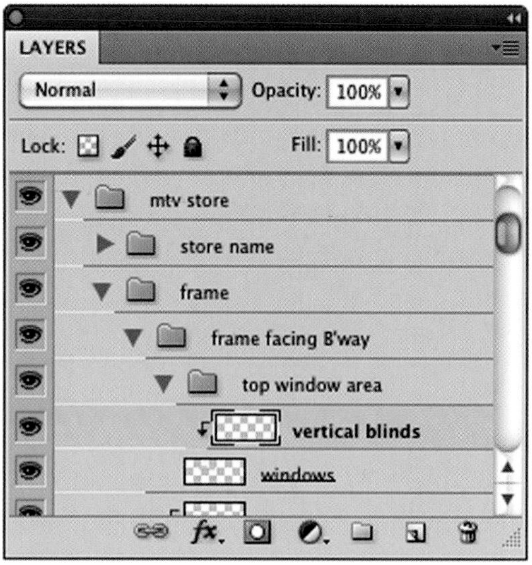

**FIG 8.5** Vertical lines (vertical blinds) clipped with window layer.

After the 3D layer was correctly positioned where it needed to be, it was then rasterized to convert it to a normal, pixel layer (3D > Rasterize). The layer was then clipped with the layer containing the shapes of the windows where the lines needed to appear (Figure 8.5).

This was accomplished by clicking between the layer of the window and the layer with the lines above it in the Layer's panel while pressing the Option key (Alt in Windows). In this case the 3D effect is so subtle, yet effective; not quite what comes to mind when you think of 3D objects.

If you needed to construct an entire 3D environment for a game, movie or such, it would be advisable to look into a 3D application that is specifically designed to handle the amount of work and detail that such a project would require. However, if you simply want to add an object to an existing scene, the tools in Photoshop are extremely capable of handling the job.

One very important thing to consider in compositing a 3D object into an existing scene is that it has to look as if it was there in the first place. Copy and paste is not enough to make it look like it belongs there. The object must interact with its environment in order to achieve the necessary realism that you might require.

Let's look at a simple 3D object created using one of the preset objects that come with Photoshop. We will then put that object into a scene and make it look like it was there when the original shot was taken. Basically we will be creating a hypothetical ad for a wine maker whose Cabernet is invading Venice. What is important to keep in mind is that it is not what is being done but rather how and why it is being done. The thought processes and the techniques are what you should concentrate on.

FIG 8.6 Scene for wine ad composite.

Figure 8.6 is a shot taken on a canal in Venice.

Figure 8.7 shows a Photoshop file where the art for our wine bottle label has been put into a layer.

With the layer containing the wine label selected, "Wine Bottle" is chosen from the 3D > New Shape From Layer menu (Figure 8.8).

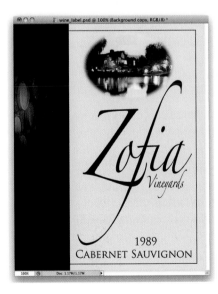

FIG 8.7 Art for wine label.

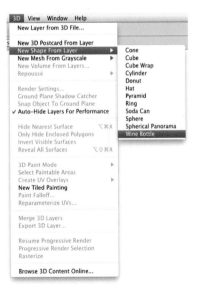

FIG 8.8 Wine label layer is converted into the preset shape "Wine Bottle".

**FIG 8.9** The result of the 3D Wine Bottle created from wine label layer.

**FIG 8.10** Wine bottle is rotated into the desired position for the ad.

The result is a rather curious looking wine bottle with the label wrapped around it (Figure 8.9).

Using the 3D Object Rotate Tool, our bottle has been spun into the position we need for the ad (Figure 8.10).

Now we need to start playing with the look of the bottle. To alter its appearance it will be necessary to call up the 3D panel from the Windows menu. In the 3D Materials section of the 3D panel, the color for the glass is changed to a deeper green to best simulate the color of a real wine bottle as seen in Figure 8.11.

The cork is another story. The cork that is generated when you choose the Wine Bottle preset is made of a solid, beige color. Color alone will not do the trick. Cork has a very specific texture and look to it. Doing a Google search for "cork," you will find tons of images. The cork image in Figure 8.12 will serve this purpose.

In the Materials section of the 3D panel the Cork Material is chosen (Figure 8.13).

Under the pull-down menu to the right of Diffuse and the swatch of the cork color, Load Texture is chosen. In the Open box that pops up, the texture for

FIG 8.11 The material for the glass portion of the bottle is colorized.

the cork is loaded. The small preview thumbnail displays the cork texture on the surface.

**Note**: Clicking on the arrow to the right of the thumbnail displays some textures that ship with Photoshop, but we want to be more precise in our look so we'll use the an imported cork texture.

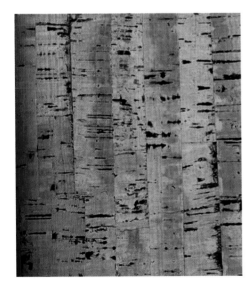

FIG 8.12 Cork texture downloaded from the web.

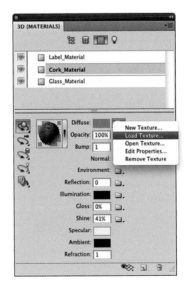

FIG 8.13 The cork texture is applied to the cork object.

**FIG 8.14** The material for the glass portion of the bottle is made transparent.

Now the glass portion of the bottle needs to look like glass. The color is right but it needs to be transparent. In the Materials section of the 3D panel, the Glass Material is chosen. The Opacity is lowered to 75%. Since the specific material was given this opacity change, the cork and label will remain completely opaque (Figure 8.14).

Next comes the lighting. Some models when generated will have light sources attached to them automatically. Some 3D models you may download from the web may contain multiple light sources. Others might have no light whatsoever. The beauty of it all is that no matter what lights an object may contain, you have total control over those lights, plus the ability to create new ones.

As in photography, how you light your subject is very important. Lighting your 3D object is equally as important. Since our 3D object is going to be placed into an existing scene it is crucial that we study the scene where the 3D object will be placed. The intensity, color and direction of the light source(s) must match or else it will look wrong. In the Venetian scene we are using for this

**FIG 8.15** The lighting for the bottle is altered to match the lighting in the scene.

chapter the sunlight is coming from the upper right, slightly behind the viewer.

When you choose the preset of Wine Bottle, the resulting model contains two infinite lights. Infinite light is a good lighting type since it is basically an ambient light source like that produced by the sun. However, there is only one sun in our solar system.

In the Lights section of the 3D panel, the second infinite light is turned off. This is done by clicking on the eye icon to the left of the light source (Figure 8.15).

**Note:** Moving the lights around is simple but you must use the tools provided in the panel. Using the 3D tools in the Tools panel will move the object.

Using the adjustment tools, the Infinite Light 1 was adjusted to point towards the bottle in the same direction as the sun in the Venetian scene.

**FIG 8.16** The render mode is set to Ray Traced Final to get the best resolution for the object.

With the bottle now complete, we switch to the Scene section of the 3D panel and set the Quality to Ray Traced Final (Figure 8.16).

This will take a few seconds but what it does is render the image as perfectly as possible within the resolution of the file.

Now the finished bottle can be exported into the Venetian scene. In Figure 8.17 you see the bottle in place.

It looks fairly believable if you wanted the bottle to float in the air. This job, however, calls for the bottle to be floating in the water.

This is where careful planning comes into play. If you are not sure what attributes your object should have, you can use any similar object from your studio or house to study how the material reacts to its environment.

We know our wine bottle is transparent glass. That effect was created within the 3D features of Photoshop. How that transparent glass will look within the new scene requires careful study of an actual glass bottle to see how it should look.

Let's take it step-by-step.

The first thing to do is to make the bottle appear to be floating in the water. Applying a layer mask to the layer will do the trick (Layer > Layer Mask > Reveal All). This adds a layer mask that is white allowing the contents to be visible. Using the Paintbrush Tool and black for the Foreground Color, the mask is painted to hide the bottom part of the bottle as seen in Figure 8.18.

**FIG 8.17** The final bottle is imported into the file with the background scene.

**FIG 8.18** The bottom portion of the bottle is masked to make the bottle appear to be floating on the water.

The glass portion of the bottle is transparent so you should be able to see the building in the background through it. Duplicate the background layer that contains the scene.

Using the Magic Wand or whatever tool works best in your situation, select the top, green glass portion of the bottle.

Make sure you are in the duplicate layer of the background and click the Add Layer Mask button at the bottom of the Layer's panel. This will make a mask that shows the contents of the layer only through the selected area.

Due to the shape of the bottle, the glass will distort what you see through it. Unlink the layer from the mask by clicking on the link icon between the layer and its mask in the Layer's panel. The reason for this is that you want to distort the contents of the layer but want to keep the mask where it is.

Still in the duplicate background layer, make sure you select the layer and not the mask for that layer. You will know you have the layer selected when the frame that surrounds the currently selected item is framing the layer, and, using the Warp Tool (Edit > Transform > Warp), twist the contents of the layer here and there to get a realistic distortion as shown in Figure 8.19.

Again, if you are not sure how this should look, pick up a real bottle and look through it to see what happens.

Next, the bottle needs to be reflected in the water.

FIG 8.19 The Background is duplicated, masked to the bottle shape and Warped to simulate the distortion caused by the shape of the glass.

FIG 8.20 The bottle layer is duplicated and flipped vertically to be used as the reflection of the bottle in the water.

Duplicate the layer of the bottle. Delete its mask and flip it vertically (Edit > Transform > Flip Vertical) as seen in Figure 8.20.

Put the layer behind the layer containing the floating bottle. Reposition it to fall directly below the bottle (Figure 8.21).

FIG 8.21 The duplicate bottle is placed in position under the original bottle.

**Notes:** Gray is used instead of black because you want the reflection to softly fade away. If black were used for the second color of the gradient then the reflection would disappear completely where the contents of the mask are black.

Since the bottle is angled backward, it is necessary to distort the reflection slightly. Using the Distort Tool (Edit > Transform > Distort), the reflection is altered to the desired result as seen in Figure 8.22.

A layer mask is applied to the layer with a gradient ranging from a gray at the bottom to white at the edge where the reflected bottle meets the floating bottle (Figure 8.23).

FIG 8.22 The reflection bottle is distorted to match the angle of the bottle it is reflecting.

FIG 8.23 A layer mask is applied to make the reflection fade as it gets further from the original bottle.

Lowering the opacity for the layer will complete this stage of the reflection as seen in Figure 8.24.

The reflection needs to be distorted by the ripples in the water. To achieve this effect the Ripple filter is applied (Filter > Distort > Ripple). In Figure 8.25 you see the particular settings that were used for this example; yours may vary. Perhaps Ocean Ripple or one of the other distortion filters will work better for your image.

The final touch for the reflection is to make it visible only through the faces of the ripples in the water that face the bottle. The faces of the ripples that face the viewer should not show the reflection. To get this tricky effect the layer styles for the reflection layer are brought into action. In the Blend If section, at the bottom of the Blending Options (Figure 8.26), the dark tones for the underlying layer are protected by moving the Dark slider until the dark tones in the water show through the reflection. Pressing the Option key (Alt in Windows), the slider is separated, making the transition between adjoining tones smoother and thus look more realistic.

What's next? A shadow. The sun is bright. You can see the shadows caused by the protrusions of the balconies on the buildings in the scene. Your bottle must also cast a shadow. The easiest way to create a shadow in this case is to give the bottle layer a layer style of Drop Shadow. Of course the resulting shadow looks like the bottle is against a picture of the scene rather than the actual place. To make the shadow look the way it should you need to separate it from the layer. Choosing Layer > Layer Style > Create Layer will put the drop

FIG 8.24 The opacity is lowered for the reflection.

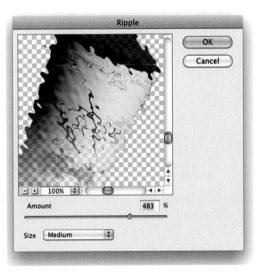

FIG 8.25 The Ripple filter gives the reflection the needed distortion caused by the rippling water.

**91**

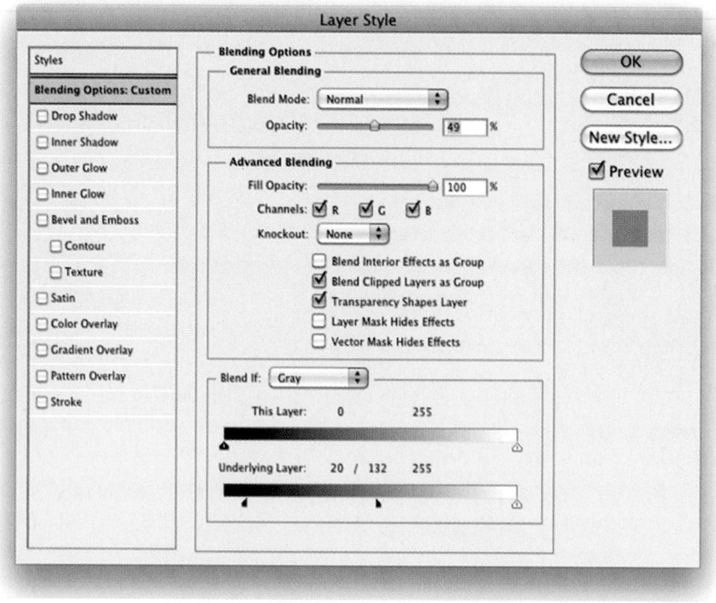

FIG 8.26 The dark tones of the underlying layer are allowed to show through to make the reflection more realistic.

shadow into its own layer behind the layer of the bottle. Now that the shadow is in its own layer it can be distorted into place as seen in Figure 8.27.

The Ripple filter is applied to the layer of the shadow using a different setting than the one used for the reflection, as shown in Figure 8.28.

FIG 8.27 The bottle is given a Drop Shadow layer style. The style is separated from the layer and distorted to match the angles in the scene.

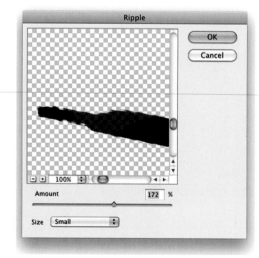

FIG 8.28 The bottle shadow layer is given the Ripple filter to match the water surface.

"Small" is used for the size because the shadow is further from us than the reflection. Lowering the opacity will complete the shadow.

Now comes the final touch — reflections on the glass. Yes the bottle is reflective just like the water, but in the case of these particular reflections, a completely different strategy must be employed.

The reflections on the bottle are mostly of elements out of the view of the image — the scene behind the viewer.

For this reflection you will resort to a new image that represents what the rest of the scene looks like behind your point of view. Accuracy is only crucial on the edge of the bottle that shows the building directly to the right of the bottle. Total accuracy? No. The end result will be so distorted it will not be noticeable. For our wine ad image we will use a different image of another canal in Venice (Figure 8.29).

FIG 8.29 A new scene will serve as the reflection of the environment on the bottle's reflective surface.

**FIG 8.30** The new scene is imported into the document with the bottle.

**FIG 8.31** The sky area is removed from the scene for the reflection.

The image is imported into the document of the wine ad. It is scaled (Edit > Transform > Scale) to a size that is close to the size of the ad as seen in Figure 8.30. What is important here is that you have enough image to distort it tightly around the bottle.

The sky area is erased from the image as shown in Figure 8.31.

FIG 8.32 The color for the scene of the reflection is desaturated.

The image is de-saturated. Using Levels (Image > Adjustments > Levels), the contrast is increased, similar to what you see in Figure 8.32.

The layer with the reflection for the bottle is clipped with the layer of the bottle (Figure 8.33).

Using the Warp Tool, the reflection is distorted to the shape of the bottle as seen in Figure 8.34.

FIG 8.33 The scene is clipped with the layer of the bottle.

FIG 8.34 The layer with the reflection is distorted to match the angles of the glass using the Warp Tool.

**FIG 8.35** The top glass portion of the bottle is selected.

**FIG 8.36** The layer with the reflection is masked through the selection of the bottle.

In the layer containing the bottle, the top, green glass area is selected (Figure 8.35).

Back in the layer containing the reflection, a layer mask is applied to the layer through the selected area. The result will show the reflection only in the glass area at the top of the bottle (Figure 8.36).

You don't want reflection over the label. Two reasons for this masking of the reflection is that the paper of the label is not reflective and, most importantly, you don't want to cover the product name.

The opacity is lowered for the layer and the result is the floating wine bottle you see in Figure 8.37.

**FIG 8.37** The final scene for the ad with the bottle floating in the water.

## 8.1. Simple Complexity

3D programs often seem so complex. Even with the simplified approach that Adobe has taken in providing 3D tools within Photoshop, it still might seem far too complex for many to get into.

To put your minds at ease, I want to show you how simple a complex job can be using the Photoshop 3D tools. You are going to create the universe! How's that for complexity?

This is an effect that you have seen many times in movies. It is an effect that took quite a bit of work and computing power to create.

In the beginning of this chapter I used the 3D Postcard feature to create a simple plane so that I could put it into 3D space. 3D Postcard From Layer is the first choice of the multiple 3D object generating functions. It is the simplest. It takes the contents of a layer and allows you to move it around in space as if it were a flat piece of art.

Using a little ingenuity you will see how this simple feature can accomplish the monumental task of creating the universe. Oh, did I forget to mention — we'll be flying through it as well? Photoshop has great animation tools, so what better segue into both animation and 3D than to fly there through space?

Start with a new file that measures 600 pixels by 600 pixels at 72 pixels per inch with a black background (Figure 8.38). Note that you are going to use this low resolution so things will happen fast. You can work at higher resolutions provided you have a powerful enough computer to handle it.

Choose the Paintbrush Tool and the fifth brush in the Panel (13). This brush tip is a hard-edged circle.

Open the Brushes panel (Window > Brushes). Here you will alter the brush to create star fields of various sized stars.

Increase the Spacing in the Brush Tip Shape section (Figure 8.39).

In the Shape Dynamics section, push the Size Jitter to 100%. Set the Minimum Diameter to 5% (Figure 8.40).

**FIG 8.38** New File with the background in black.

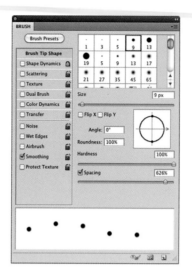

FIG 8.39 The Spacing for the brush tips is increased in the Brushes panel.

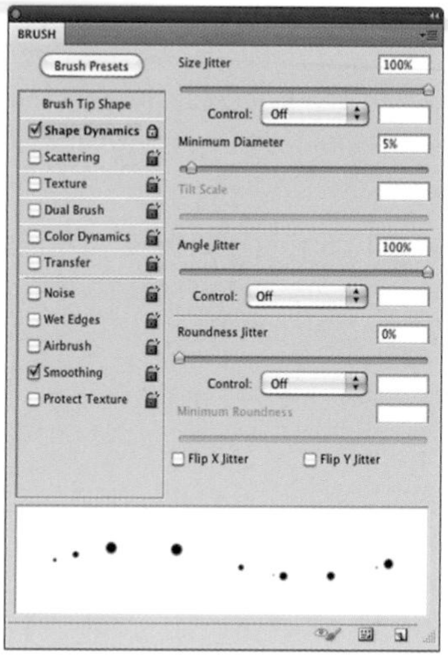

FIG 8.40 The Shape Dynamics is altered.

In the Scattering section, push the Scatter on Both Axis to 1000%. Raise the Count to 2 and the Count Jitter to 100% (Figure 8.41).

Create a new, blank layer.

Using white for the Foreground color, stroke the canvas with the brush you just created. The result should be a loosely spaced stroke like the one seen in Figure 8.42. You want it to look airy.

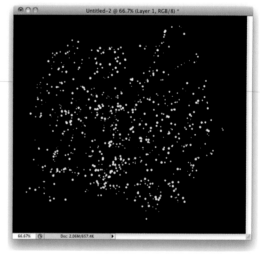

FIG 8.41 The Scattering is applied to the brush tips.

FIG 8.42 In a layer, a star field is created.

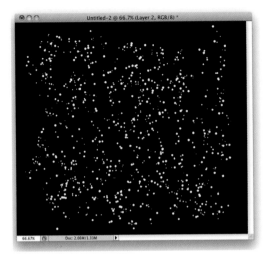

FIG 8.43 A second star field is created.

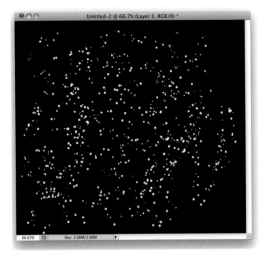

FIG 8.44 A third star field is created.

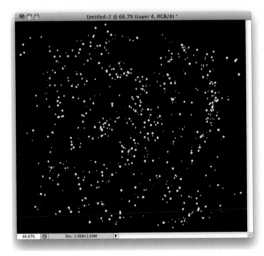

FIG 8.45 A fourth star field is created.

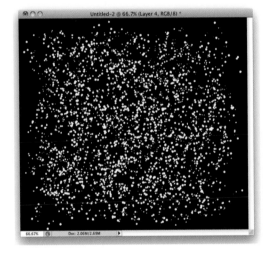

FIG 8.46 All four star field layers over each other.

Create three more layers that contain similar strokes like the ones seen in Figures 8.43–8.45.

Figure 8.46 shows the four layers laying over each other in the file.

Convert each layer into a 3D Postcard (3D > New 3D Postcard From Layer).

You want all four layers to work as one. In order to achieve this, select two layers and choose Merge 3D Layers from the 3D menu. You can only merge two layers at a time. Once two are merged, merge them to the third and then to the fourth.

FIG 8.47 The merged 3D layers are rotated onto their sides.

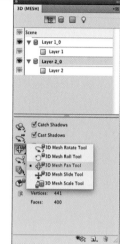

FIG 8.48 3D Mesh Pan Tool in the 3D panel.

Now that all four layers are merged into one, using the Object Rotate Tool from the Tool panel, rotate the layers towards you as shown in Figure 8.47.

You will now separate the four layers from each other to increase the distance between them.

Select the layer that is at the top of the stack. The first layer you created (Layer 1) should be at the top of the list.

Using the Mesh Pan Tool from the list of tools found in the 3D panel (**Note**: Mesh Pan is in the group that has the Mesh Rotate Tool visible by default as shown in Figure 8.48), move the layer up, away from the rest of the stack (Figure 8.49).

FIG 8.49 The topmost layer is moved up to separate it from the stack.

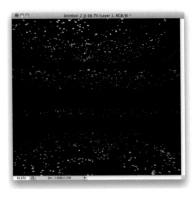

FIG 8.50 The space between all four layers is increased.

Select the second layer and move it up so it is centered between the top layer and the rest of the stack.

Select the fourth layer and move it down so that all four layers are equidistant to each other (Figure 8.50).

Using the Object Rotate Tool from the Tool panel, rotate the layers back to their original, upright position as shown in Figure 8.51.

You will notice that they don't look exactly as they did in Figure 8.46 before they were adjusted. This is because two of the layers are closer to you and one is farther than the original view.

Open the Animation panel (Window > Animation).

Click the arrow for Layer 1, the 3D object, to expose the controls (Figure 8.52).

FIG 8.51 The final 3D star field ready to be animated.

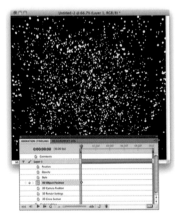

FIG 8.52 In the Animation panel a keyframe is created.

**FIG 8.53** The 3D Object Slide Tool in the Tools panel.

Click on the tiny stopwatch icon for the 3D Object Position. This will create a keyframe for the animation.

Move the Current Time Indicator (small, blue triangle in the timeline) over to the end of the animation time sequence.

Using the Object Slide Tool from the Tool panel (Figure 8.53), move the layers towards you.

**Note:** Clicking in the center and dragging downward will move the object towards the viewer.

When you have moved it close enough so the star fields look similar to the ones in Figure 8.54, release the mouse button.

A new keyframe will automatically appear at the end of the animation where the Current Time Indicator was placed.

Rewind the animation, sit back and watch. The first time it loads into memory so it runs a little slow. The second time you watch it... well, do it.

Add a few titles and you now have a great intro to your movie!

Throughout this book you learn many ways to create and manipulate 3D objects. They are beautiful! Once you try 3D in Photoshop, the real fun starts!

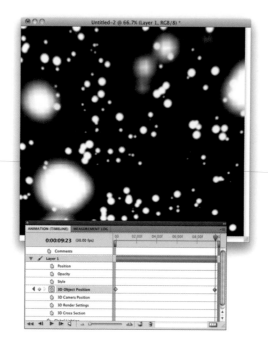

**FIG 8.54** The final animation ready to be played.

# CHAPTER 9

# Adobe Repoussé with Corey Barker

Well, at this point in the book you have no doubt discovered that 3D in Photoshop is an extremely powerful new feature; one that I believe is a game changer for anyone working in Photoshop, especially if you are a designer. While some 3D features have been available in Photoshop in the last couple versions, getting really involved, seemingly complex 3D art (like the 3D art you will see in this chapter) into Photoshop would have involved another 3D application in which you would have had to export the 3D art then import into Photoshop as a regular layer. This would have meant that if you wanted to make changes you would have had to go back to the 3D app then re-import back to Photoshop. And on top of all that, dedicated 3D applications are hard to learn.

Repoussé brings a whole new level of 3D into Photoshop, allowing you to create 3D text, objects, and abstract elements all without leaving Photoshop. The best part is that it is easy to learn. In this chapter we will examine the numerous ways you can create different types of 3D objects and then combine them to create a complete 3D environment

**3D in Photoshop. DOI: 10.1016/B978-0-240-81377-6.10009-2**

all within Photoshop. Now as we progress through these lessons you will see that 3D requires you to think a little differently in Photoshop. While Photoshop may have always been a two-dimensional application, going into that third dimension can be confusing for some; so throughout this chapter I have added some of my workflow suggestions to help your work go smoother. One thing I stress throughout is to save often. You have no doubt heard this before but with 3D I feel it's more important. You only have to spend an hour building some cool 3D art and then have it crash without saving once and you will never do it again. Trust me!

With that, let us press on with our Photoshop 3D journey by starting with a simple exercise of building 3D elements from scratch and applying simple reflection and shadow effects.

## 9.1. Text and Reflections

In this exercise we will take a look at creating 3D elements from vector paths and text to create a metallic looking film reel with a title. I have always made it a habit to build elements in separate documents and then bring them together into a finished design file. It especially makes sense with 3D since the center point of a 3D layer is determined by the center of the document. So if you have more of a rectangular document the perspective of your 3D object will be slightly off.

**Step 1**: Open the film_reel.psd file and open the Paths panel to locate the saved path shape of the film reel. Grab the Path selection tool on the toolbar and select the entire film reel path.

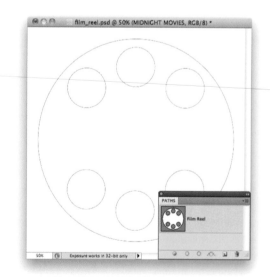

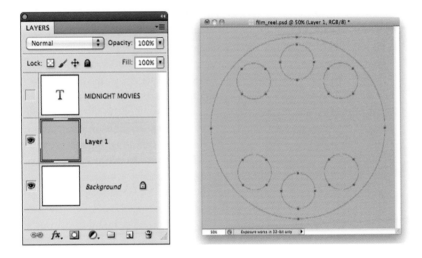

**Step 2**: Now go into the Layers panel and create a new blank layer. Open the Swatches panel and choose the pure yellow orange color swatch. Then fill the new layer with this new color by pressing Option-Delete (Windows: Alt-Backspace).

**Step 3**: With the path selected, go to the Window menu and choose 3D to open the 3D panel. You should see the Create New 3D Object section of the panel. Under the source menu choose Work Path and check on 3D Repoussé Object. Then click the Create button to open the Repoussé panel.

You will notice that a default extrusion of the shape has been applied but the holes in the reel are filled in. There is a quick and easy fix for this.

**Step 4**: At the bottom of the Repoussé panel there is a section called Internal Constraints. Among the many functions of this small section, one of the most common is perhaps knocking out holes in shapes — in this case the reel holes. Go into the Type menu and change the setting from Inactive to Hole. This will knock out one of the shapes. You will then need to select one of the tools to the left of the menu and use it to select the remaining holes. As you drag the cursor over the shapes they will be highlighted. Simply click once to select then go into the Type menu once again and change the setting from Inactive to Hole again. Do this to all the remaining holes in the shape. Don't click OK yet.

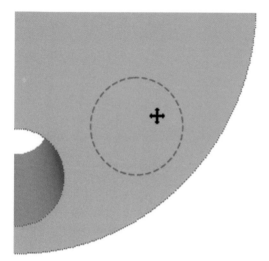

**Step 5**: In the Repoussé panel go up to the Extrude section and set the Depth to .1 to make the film reel a bit thinner. You can use the mesh tools on the side of the panel to modify the position of the shape as you edit the Repoussé settings, but I would recommend that when you are done editing click the Home button at the bottom to set back to the original position then click OK. This will ensure that no matter how much you change the 3D object with the 3D tools you can always click the Home button in the options bar to return to the original position. Now click OK.

Here is a good place to save your work.

**Step 6**: Now that we have the reel created we need to create the text element. Here I have a text layer with the words MIDNIGHT MOVIES set in a font called Eurostile and filled with gray. It is ultimately going to be filled with the same yellow color of the reel but I am using gray for the sake of visibility. With the text layer selected, go under the 3D menu, go to Repoussé and choose Text Layer.

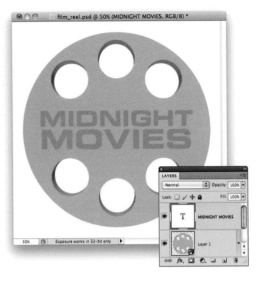

Just as before, it will apply a default extrusion and open the Repoussé panel. In the Extrude section set the Depth to .5. Then go over to the Bevel section and set the Height and Width to 2. Also once again click the Home button to set the original position and click OK.

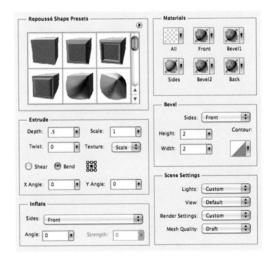

**Step 7**: Now we have two 3D Repoussé layers we need to merge together. Merging them will not flatten the art; it will simply group multiple 3D objects into a single 3D layer. Select both the layers in the Layers panel. Go to the 3D menu and choose Merge 3D Layers.

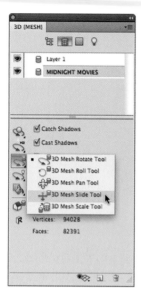

**Step 8**: Often when you merge 3D layers, objects tend to shift around. Sometimes objects will be hiding behind other shapes. Open the 3D panel and click the second icon at the top to open the Mesh panel. Highlight the text mesh in the list that is the same name as the layer. Then just below to the left there are a number of different 3D tools. Click on the Mesh Tool icon (third one down) and hold to reveal all the mesh tools. Choose the 3D Mesh Slide Tool. Now when you move your cursor over the canvas you will notice the tool is context sensitive. Place a box around the mesh as you drag over it. This will override whatever you have selected in the mesh list so be careful. Click on the text then click and drag down to bring the text forward.

**Step 9**: Now, with the text in place, we can change the color to match the rest of the graphic. Open the Layers panel and you will see some sub-layers attached to the master 3D layer. These contain the textures for the shapes. Double-click the MIDNIGHT MOVIES layer to open the texture file.

When it opens you will see the original text in gray. Instead of filling the text create a new blank layer and fill it with the same pure yellow orange we used on the reel graphic. You do not have to flatten the image as the texture files will support layered documents. Close the document and save the changes and the color of the text will be updated.

**Step 10**: Now we have our 3D elements created, let's add some environmental elements to enhance the realism a bit more. Don't worry about shadows yet — we will get to that. Open the 3D panel and click on the Materials section (third icon over). At the top, you will see a list of all the material surfaces in the layer. What we want to do here is add a reflective environment to some of the surfaces of this shape. To do this, we need to select the material surface first. First highlight the Layer 1 Front Inflation Material. This is the front of the reel graphic. Go to the bottom part of the panel to the Environment setting. Click on the folder icon next to it and choose Load Texture. When the windows open locate whatever texture file you want to use. Here I have a cool black and white graphic of a film called "environment.jpg" to go along with the movie theme. Click OK.

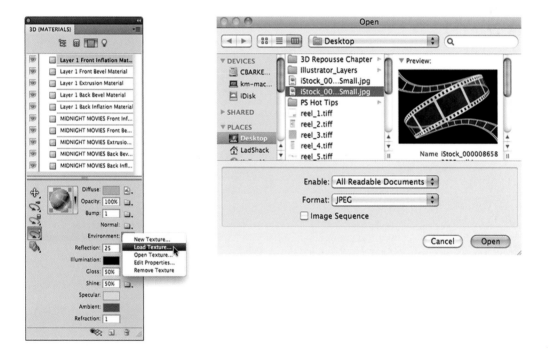

**Step 11**: Now set the Reflection property just below that to 25%. This setting can be adjusted; you may want to start at a low setting. Also set the Gloss and Shine properties just below that to 50%.

**Step 12**: Repeat the last two steps on the Layer 1 Extrusion and also on the Midnight Movies Front Inflation and the Midnight Movies Extrusion to finish off the shiny reflective look on the whole graphic.

I would save again right here.

**Step 13**: Now create a new document to place the 3D elements into. Since we used a square document to create the 3D object we can now take this into the final design. Here I created a wide format document at 12" × 6.75" and set the background to black by pressing Command-I (PC: Ctrl-I). Then go to the 3D file and grab the layer in the Layers panel and drag it into the new file. Hold the Shift key as you drag it over to make it drop in the center.

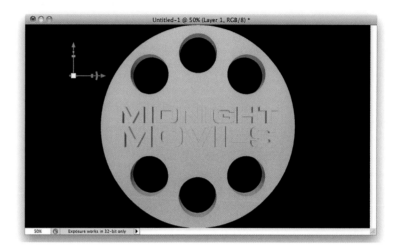

**Step 14**: Click and hold on the 3D Object Rotate Tool to reveal all the other tools and choose 3D Object Slide Tool. Then click inside the canvas and drag down to slide the whole 3D object forward. This the cool part about compositing in 3D in that you can slide your object back and forth, side to side, on any axis to get the best composition. Here I want the graphic really close in so use the slide to bring it forward and tilt it slightly. Feel free to experiment and get used to the way the tools work and feel.

**Step 15:** One last thing… if you remember earlier I mentioned shadows. They are there, but we can't see them because of the Draft render mode we are working in. When we created the 3D objects, Photoshop put some default lights on them. You can see them by going into the 3D panel and clicking on the light bulb icon at the top. This will reveal all the Light settings. You can see from the list of light types that we have three infinite lights on this subject. Modifying the position of these lights can change the overall appearance of the object; notice that among the other 3D tools in the panel there is a light set of the tools. These allow you to change just the lights.

Editing lights can be a bit tricky because it's not a solid shape. What you need to do is go to the bottom of the 3D panel and you will see the eyeball and the grid icon. Click on this and select 3D light.

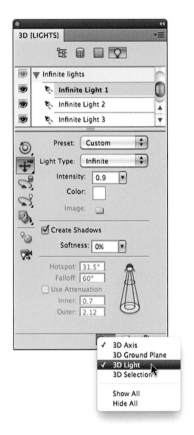

This will reveal the wire frame of the light so you can edit easier. Select a light from the list and click and drag around the canvas to change the light direction. You will see the lighting of the scene change as you drag around. You can turn lights off or change the intensity right here in the Light panel.

Now would be a good time to save!

**Step 16**: With the lights in place, go into the 3D panel one last time and click on the first icon at the top to access the Scene settings. Go down to the quality menu and choose Ray Traced Draft. This will execute a rough render complete with more reflections and shadows.

If all looks well then go ahead and do a final render or continue to tweak the graphic with all the tools we have used thus far.

## 9.2. Creating Realistic 3D Product Shots

In this tutorial we are going to explore Photoshop's 3D tools even further by creating a 3D product shot from a 2D image. Another tremendous advantage of these new features is the ability to apply extrusions to images. Pretty much anything that is on a layer can be made 3D — it just depends on how far you want to take it.

**Step 1**: For this exercise, all we need is a flat two-dimensional image of the product. In this case it's a smart phone product. You can choose to follow this exercise along with the supplied image if you wish but make sure you experiment with other images. You will need to extract whatever product shot you use from its background or at least have a good selection made around it. If the image is extracted, as it is here, then hold down the Command key (Windows: Ctrl) and right-click on the layer icon to load it as a selection.

**Step 2**: Go under the 3D menu and go to Repoussé and select Current Selection. This will apply a default extrusion to the selected shape and open the Repoussé panel. You can use the mesh tools in the Repoussé window to change the orientation of the object as you make changes. Go into the Extrude section and change the Depth to 0.1. Then go over to the Bevel section and set the Height to 2 and the Width to 3. This will help give the product a more realistic edge. Also, to clean up the edges a bit, go to the Scene settings just below and change Mesh Quality to Better. When done, click the Home button at the bottom of the tools to set the object back to its original position. Click OK.

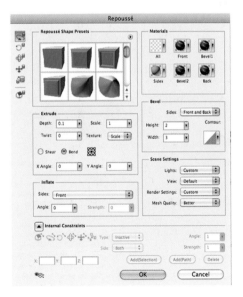

**Step 3**: Now we need to change the color of the sides. By default, Repoussé filled it with a neutral gray. If you grab the 3D Object Rotate Tool from the toolbar you can rotate the object to get a better view of the sides. We need the sides to be the same color as the rest of the phone. Grab the Eyedropper Tool from the toolbar and click in the dark gray area of the phone to sample the color.

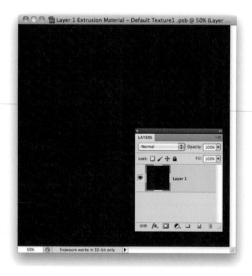

Now open the Layers panel. Select the layer that contains the product. You will notice there are smaller sub-layers attached to the main layer. These contain the texture files for each of the surfaces of the 3D layer. Double-click the Layer 1 Extrusion Material to open the texture file as a separate document. Then fill this file with the sampled dark gray color. Close the document and save the changes. Then return to the original document and the sides should update automatically.

**Step 4**: Notice on the sides there is a little bit of a white edge that is a bit distracting. Here's a quick fix for that. Go into the Layers panel again and open the Layer 1 sub-layer that contains the phone face. Double-click to open. Then create a new blank layer right under the product layer and fill with the same dark gray you filled the sides with. You do not have to flatten texture images like this for 3D layers. They will support multi-layered texture files. That's a big help! Close the document and save the changes.

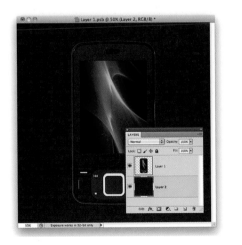

Notice that back in the original file you'll see those little white edges magically disappear. Use the 3D tools once again to move the object around to see if all the sides are good. You can also change view by selecting a position angle in the options bar or use the Axis Widget in the canvas. When done, click the Home button in the options bar again to reset the object back to its original position.

This is a good place to save your work. I will mention this often as working with 3D can be very processor intensive and you don't want to have to redo a complex piece of 3D art all over again.

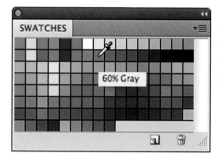

**Step 5**: Now click create a new blank layer under the current 3D layer. Hold down the Command key (Windows: Ctrl) and click the New Layer icon at the bottom of the Layers panel to create a new layer under the current layer. Open the Swatches panel and choose the 60% gray swatch.

**Step 6**: Press the letter D to set the default colors. Then select the Gradient Tool on the toolbar. Go into the options bar and click on the gradient preview. Click the first icon to select the Foreground to Background. Then choose the Radial gradient type next to the preview.

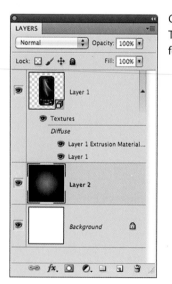

Click in the middle of the canvas and drag to the edge of the document. This will give a subtle gray Radial gradient. This will be the ground plane for the product. The gradient just enhances the lighting a bit.

**Step 7**: Now we need to make this image a 3D layer as well. This time, however, we are only going to need this to be a 3D postcard. Go under the 3D menu and choose New 3D Postcard From Layer.

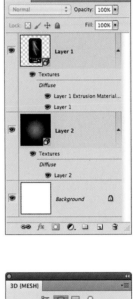

**Step 8**: What you should have at this point is a layer containing the phone and the ground plane layer. Select both of these layers and go under the 3D menu once more and choose Merge 3D Layers. This doesn't flatten the layers, it merely places both 3D objects into a single 3D layer.

**Step 9**: Go under the Window menu and choose 3D to open the 3D panel. Click on the second icon to open the Mesh section of the 3D panel. At the top of this section there is a list of all the meshes contained in this layer. You can change the name of these to help you. Here I changed them to Ground Plane and Phone. This way I know exactly what I am working on. Select the Ground Plane mesh and go down along the left side of the panel and you will see the various 3D tools. Go to the third one down which is the mesh tools. Click and hold to reveal all the mesh tools and choose the 3D Mesh Rotate Tool. These tools will manipulate the individual meshes located in an object whereas the main 3D rotate tools rotate the entire object as whole.

**Step 10**: You can rotate the ground plane manually if you want just by click and dragging up, but to make the ground plane perpendicular to the phone you can go into the options bar and enter 90 or −90 into the X Orientation.

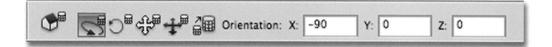

**Step 11**: Go back into the mesh tools and choose the 3D Mesh Pan Tool. Then click and drag down to bring the ground plane down to the bottom of the phone so it appears to be sitting on the surface. Now here is where some practice will help. Working in the third dimension in Photoshop requires rather different thinking when editing. When editing a layer with multiple meshes like this you can select the meshes in the Mesh 3D panel or, if you have a mesh tool selected, you can drag over a mesh in the canvas and it will highlight the mesh object with a wireframe, giving you the ability to jump from one mesh to the other without going to the panel every time. For example, after the ground plane was in place, I used the Mesh Scale Tool to increase the size of the ground plane by clicking on the mesh and dragging to scale down. If you need to scale up simply click and drag up. Use the other mesh tools to scale, slide, and position the phone on the surface of the ground plane.

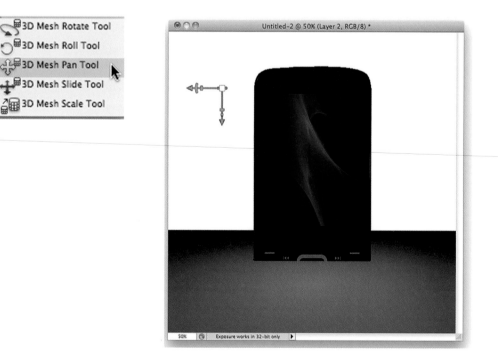

**Step 12**: So we now have our 3D object sitting on a 3D plane. Now we need lights. Right now the product is very hard to see so we need to illuminate the product with some 3D lights. Open the 3D panel again and click on the last icon at the top that looks like a light bulb. This is where you manage the lights. You can add four different kinds of lights. In this case we are going to use a couple of spot lights to add some drama to the layout.

Click on the new icon at the bottom of the panel and choose New Spotlight. You may see part of the image brighten up depending on where the light appears, but the light is pretty hard to see when trying to position it. At the bottom of the panel there is an icon with an eye and a grid. This is where you can turn on wireframes for the lights so you can see where they are pointing. Click on the menu and choose 3D Light to see the spotlight wireframe.

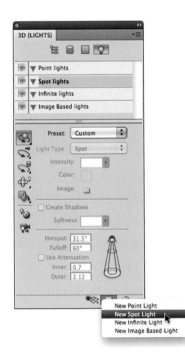

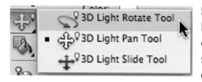

**Step 13**: Now just below the mesh tools in the 3D panel are the light tools. These work the same way as the mesh tools only they change the lights and, like the meshes, lights are also context sensitive meaning you can hover over the lights to select them or choose them in the panel list.

Using 3D lights is also something that only gets easy with practice. I can only really describe how I place them, but you really need to try it and see how they behave; this is something that benefits you in the long run as you will be using lights a lot. I promise.

What we want to do here, in this case, is put the light directly above the phone itself, so use the 3D Light Rotate Tool to point the light down. Then use the 3D Light Pan Tool to drag the light up beyond the boundaries of the document. Don't go too far as the light intensity drops off the further away it is from the subject. If you want, you can make the light brighter simply by changing the Intensity setting in the Light panel. I also added a second light to illuminate the left side of the product a little bit more.

**Step 14**: Now, with the lights in place, we need to change the angle of the phone. However we can't really use the object rotate tools to change the angle. The reason for this is that when you rotate an object with the 3D Object Rotate Tool it will rotate the object but not the lights. So if you change the object angle the lighting will change. The way to change the angle of an object without changing the lighting is to use the 3D camera tools. Select the 3D Rotate Camera Tool and click and rotate around the view of the image. Notice that the angle changes and the lights change with it because you are changing your angle of view rather than the object itself. In this image I placed the camera to the lower left side of the phone, giving it a more commanding presence. You can see that it's probably a good habit to use the cameras more when you have a really complex 3D layer with numerous lights.

Good time to save here.

**Step 15**: Next open up the file that will be the background image. Take this image and drag and drop it into the main design file. Then position this layer just under the main 3D product layer.

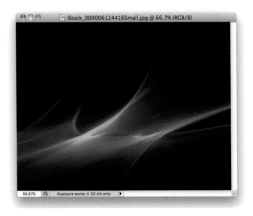

**Step 16**: Now we need to set up the reflections on all the surfaces. Open the 3D panel and click on the third icon over to open the Materials section. In the list select Layer 2, which contains the ground plane. Go down to the Reflection property and set it to 25%. You will not see any change to your image because some reflections need to be rendered. We'll get to that.

**Step 17**: Next select the Layer 1 Inflation Material and go down and set the Reflection to 5%. Then click on the folder icon next to Environment. When the menu pops up choose Load Texture. Then locate the same file we used for the background and click Open. If you move the camera around you will see the image reflected in the front surface. Get the final positioning of the camera to where you can see a fair amount of the reflection.

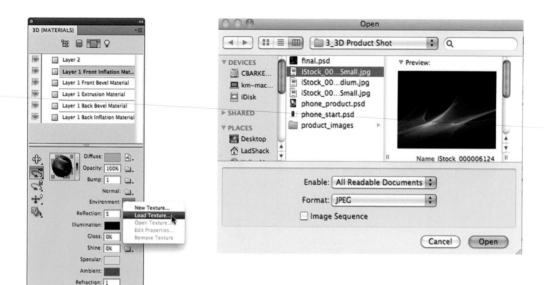

**Step 18**: Repeat Step 17 on the sides of the phone, which is the Layer 1 Extrusion Material. Only set the Reflection amount a little bit higher this time, around 10%.

**Step 19**: Now here is a little tiny thing. I can see that the image looks pretty good. Only thing is the ground plane looks odd now. It needs color. Go into the Layers panel and double-click the Layer 2 that contains the ground plane texture. Once open, set a simple Hue/Saturation adjustment layer to give the layer color. Click Colorize in the Adjustment panel and set the Hue to 205 and the Saturation to 75. Then close the document and save the changes. The new color plane should be updated.

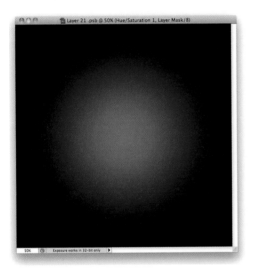
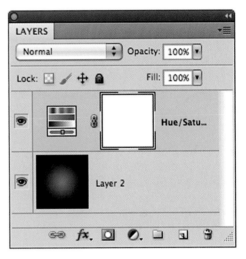

**Step 20**: Now it's time to do a rough render. Open the 3D panel and click on the first icon to open the Scene section. Make sure that scene is selected at the top of the list and go to the Quality menu in the middle of the panel and choose Ray Traced Draft. This will do a basic render of the elements revealing the shadows and reflections. You can pause the render at any time by pressing any button. Once you make a change the render will start back up automatically. It will continue to render as long as you have Ray Traced Draft or Ray Traced Final selected in the Quality menu. You can also go under the 3D menu and choose Resume Progressive Render.

**Note**: You may want to change the Mesh Quality setting we changed in Step 2 to Best. Remember, you can get back into the Repoussé settings for the phone by going into the Mesh section of the 3D panel, selecting the mesh containing the phone, then clicking the R icon at the bottom left under the tools.

Finally… SAVE!!!

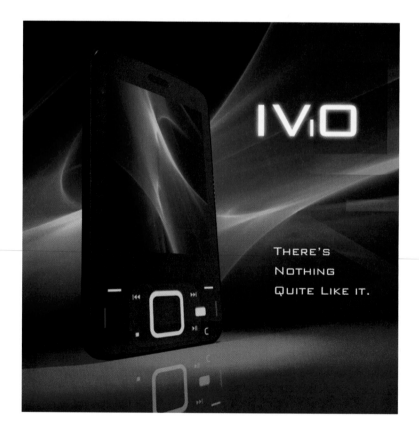

## 9.3. Masking 3D Shapes for Effect

Here is another cool way to take advantage of the 3D features in Photoshop CS5. So many 3D effects use obvious 3D shapes and that works great, but you can also use shapes to carry a certain type of effect. In this case we are going to make the extrusion material of a text object appear as though it has a light burst coming through the text. It will give you a good idea of how creative you can get just masking a shape.

**Step 1**: Start by creating a new document 9"W × 5"H at 100 ppi, then select the Text tool in the toolbar. Click in the canvas to set a text layer and type the word or words you want to apply the effect to. Here I chose TITAN in a special stylized font.

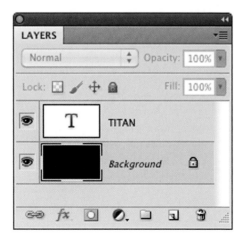

**Step 2**: This technique calls for some unusual approaches. Before we apply Repoussé to this layer we need to flip it around. It will make sense later. Go under the Edit menu to Transform and choose Flip Horizontal.

**Step 3**: With the text layer still selected, go into the 3D menu to Repoussé and choose Text Layer. Set the Extrusion Depth to 5 and the Scale to 5 as well. (Remember: applying Repoussé to a text layer will rasterize the text. So it may be a good idea to duplicate the text layer.) This will extrude the text back and make it larger at one end than the other by 500%. Use the mesh tools to move around the object to see the extrusion if you like but remember to click the Home button to return to original position. Click OK.

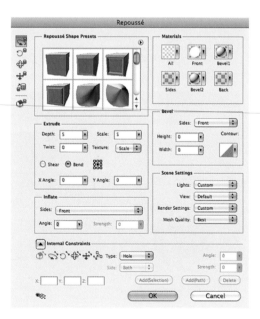

**Step 4**: Now we need to flip the text back around so it will read right. Except we cannot flip it the way we did before because the text is a 3D object now. Go into the toolbar and select the 3D Object Rotate Tool. Then go up into the options bar and enter 180 in the Z orientation.

Now would perhaps be a good time to save your work.

**Step 5**: Go into the Window menu and choose 3D to open the 3D panel. Open the Materials section and in the materials list locate the TITAN Back Inflation Material and select it. Then, just below, enter 0 in the Opacity setting. This will make the back face, which is actually the front of the text, invisible.

**Step 6**: Next, locate and select the TITAN Extrusion Material. Go to the Opacity setting again and this time click on the small folder icon and choose New Texture from the menu. A new document window will pop up. Go ahead and make this new document the same size as the working file. Click OK.

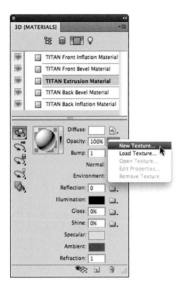

**Step 7**: Now you notice it did not open the file. It just created the new document and attached it to the Opacity property. We need to now open the file by clicking on the menu next to Opacity once again and then choosing Open Texture from the menu.

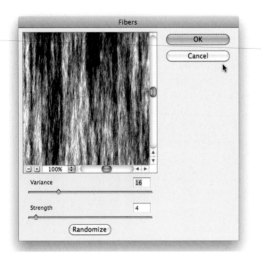

**Step 8**: This new Opacity file works the same way a layer mask works in Photoshop. It's just in 3D and is a separate file rather than attached to the layer. However it does use black to hide areas, white to reveal, and gray areas show some transparency. What we are after here is a light burst effect coming out of the text.

Press D to set the toolbar colors to default black & white. Then go under the Filter menu and go to Render and choose Fibers. Go ahead and use the default settings and click OK.

Now go under the Filter menu again and go to Blur and choose Motion Blur. Set the Angle to 90 so the blur is going straight up and down and set the Distance to around 400. This will give you smooth varying gray streaks. Click OK.

**Step 9**: Now go into the toolbar and grab the Gradient Tool. In the options bar click on the gradient preview and choose Foreground to Transparent gradient. Make sure black is set as the foreground color. Click to start the gradient at the bottom of the image. Hold the Shift key down and drag up close to the top of the document.

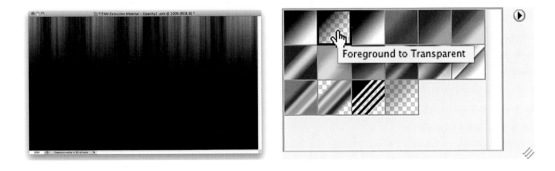

**Step 10**: If the light beams still seem a little too light just make a quick Levels adjustment. Go under the Image menu to Adjustments and choose Levels. Here I just set the Highlight Output level to 175; this will darken the overall image rather than introducing a lot of contrast. Click OK.

**Step 11**: Close this document and save the changes. Back in the original file you will immediately see the light burst effect start to appear, but it needs a few more tweaks to get it just right. There are some default features we need to turn off. Open the 3D panel and go to the Mesh section. Uncheck Catch Shadows and Cast Shadows.

Here also would be a good place to save!

**Step 12**: Go into the Materials section of the 3D panel and highlight the TITAN Front Inflation Material. Move down to the settings and you will see Color Swatches next to Diffuse, Illumination, Specular, and Ambient. Change all of these to white. Do this for the Front Inflation as well as the Extrusion Material. This will eliminate any dirty light noise that may appear.

**Step 13**: Now the light burst looks pretty good but we are going to enhance it a bit using a layer style. With the 3D layer selected go into the Layers panel and click on the Layer Style menu at the bottom and choose Outer Glow from the menu.

When the Outer Glow window opens, go into the Structure section and click on the color swatch and change the color to white, then set the Opacity to 50%. Move down to the Elements section and set the Size to 20. These settings work for this scenario but you may need to tweak your settings if you are using different text or artwork. Click OK when done.

**Step 14**: We certainly could have built this graphic in color but I chose to build black on white because that will allow me to use an adjustment layer to change the color on the fly. Simply go into the Adjustment layer menu and choose Hue/Saturation. Check Colorize and set the Hue to 30 and the Saturation to 75. This will give the overall text object a yellow/gold look.

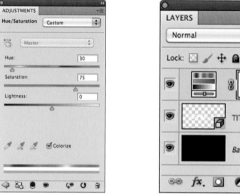

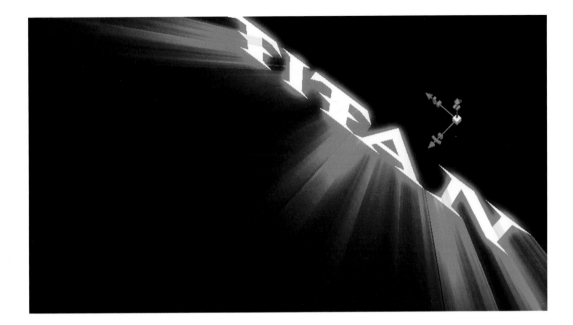

At this point save your work again. Then feel free to use the 3D object tools to rotate the object at different angles. Notice how the light burst looks cool pretty much from any angle, giving numerous compositional possibilities with a single 3D object. You can also change the color in the adjustment layer to get an entirely different look altogether.

## 9.4. 3D and Photoshop Effects

As I have mentioned before, one of the biggest advantages of having 3D capabilities in Photoshop is that we are always in Photoshop; meaning we have all the cool features that Photoshop offers along with the 3D features to create really eye-popping 3D art. In this exercise we will take a look at an image that I created, and which was eventually made into the lenticular poster inserted in this book.

I will start first by showing how I set up the image to create the 3D elements. I began with the main CS5 letter of the image. Since there were only three letters I went ahead and made each letter on a separate text layer.

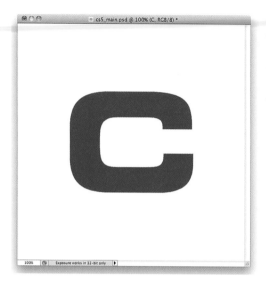

**Step 1**: Create a new square document. Again, a square format ensures that the center point of the 3D object in relation to the file dimensions is even. I set the first text layer with the letter C in a font called Eurostile Bold Extended and then chose a dark blue color for the color fill.

**Step 2**: To keep all the same formatting for the additional text layers just make a duplicate of the C layer by pressing Command-J (Ctrl-J). Then highlight the text with the Text Tool and change it to S. Do this again for the 5.

**Step 3**: Apply Repoussé to each of the text layers. I used an Extrusion Depth of 0.6 and set the Bevel Height to 2 and the Width to 3. Apply these same settings to each layer.

Next go into the 3D panel to the Materials section and set the Front Inflation Material and the Extrusion Material to 25%. Then merge them into a single 3D layer. Remember you can only merge two 3D layers at a time so don't select all three at once.

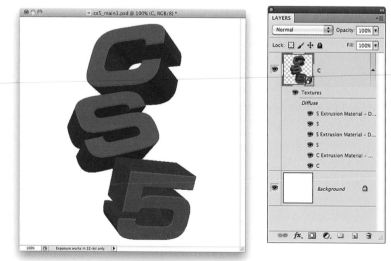

**Note**: If the extrusion material did not pick up the blue color of the text you can simply go into the Layers panel and open the extrusion texture file and fill with the right color.

**Step 4**: When done, use the object mesh tools in the 3D panel to rotate and reposition the letters so they are stacked on top of each other as you see here.

When done, save this document and move it out of the way for now.

**Step 5**: Now create a new document that is 15"W × 7"H. For this part we are going to create the scattered letters at the bottom of the image. While they appear to be random, it's actually the word REPOUSSE hiding in plain sight. So with that it starts with typing Repoussé on a new text layer in the same font and color we used for the CS5.

**Note**: If you want to type the accent on the second E in Repoussé, on a Mac hold down the OPTION key and press E, and then press E again. In Windows, hold down Alt and press 1, 3 and then 0.

**Step 6**: Now with CS5 being only made up of three letters, making a separate layer for each was no big deal. However making a separate layer for each letter in Repoussé would require a few layers and a bit more work. So we are going to make it easier by turning the entire word into a Repoussé object with an Extrusion Depth of 0.5.

**Step 7**: At this point you can choose to continue to build this element in this original file, but I would rather use the document I am going to build the final design in. This way I know exactly what will be visible in the image. So I built the image in a document 8"W × 9"H at 300 ppi and then brought over the Repoussé text.

**Step 8**: We need to be able to reposition all the letters in a way that looks relatively random. However, if you were to grab the 3D Rotate Tool and rotate the 3D object now, it would rotate the word as a uniform shape. To break the letters go under the 3D menu and go to Repoussé and select Split Repoussé Meshes. This will make each unattached element a separate mesh object. In this case, each letter is a separate mesh object.

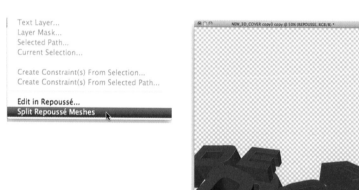

**Step 9**: Now use the object mesh tools in the 3D panel to rotate and reposition the letters around the bottom. You want to be aware, especially in the case of lenticular, that there are elements that are close and others far away. Managing multiple 3D shapes can take some getting used to, but the fact that you can hover over a shape and change it without going into the 3D panel every time is a huge time saver. With all the elements in place let's move on to abstract elements.

**Step 10**: The last 3D elements to be added are the yellow electric cords. These add a more enhanced 3D appearance as well as carrying the lightning effect we will be adding shortly. These cords started as four simple shapes on a colored layer. With the four shapes selected go under the 3D menu and go to Repoussé and choose Selected Path.

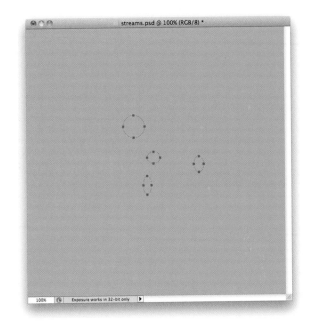

Inside the Repoussé panel set the Extrusion Depth to 10. Then set the Scale to 0.2. This will make the cords taper as they recede in space, enhancing the perspective. Just below the Depth setting set the Twist property to 400. Just below that make sure you have Bend checked on and then set the X angle to 150. This will make the cords bend on a curve and the twisting will add an element of chaos to the shapes. Also make sure that you have your Mesh Quality set to Best since this geometry contains many bends and twists where smaller triangles (Best Mesh Quality) will give smoother results. Click OK.

**Step 11:** The extrude sides are still gray by default. Simply go into the Layers panel and double-click on the extrusion texture layer and fill with the same yellow color from before.

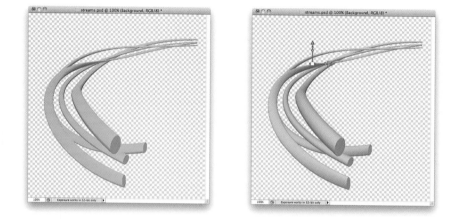

**Step 12:** One thing to note, and this is a good example of being able to edit 3D after the fact, is the yellow bevels on the CS5 letters. I decided on that right at the end to help define the letters more and to differentiate them from the background. All you do is locate the mesh in the Materials section of the 3D panel and click on the R at the bottom of the panel.

Then go into the Materials section of the Repoussé panel and click on the Side menu and choose a yellow texture from the list. Click OK

**Step 13:** With the elements created, we can now bring them together. We already have the Repoussé letter in the layout, so go and get the CS5 object and bring that into the layout and position just above the scattered letters. Next bring in the yellow cords. Then make a couple of duplicates of this layer so we can add them in a couple places.

**Step 14**: At this point I am looking at about seven 3D layers. In order to take advantage of reflections and shadows we need to merge all of these 3D layers into one. I would recommend merging two layers, positioning the newly merged item, then doing the next. Items will shift around greatly as you merge so be mindful that some objects are hiding behind others.

**Step 15**: When you are done merging you are going to need to make sure all the visible surfaces are going to be reflective. Open the 3D panel and go to the Materials section. At this point the list will be long but you will need to make sure at least that all the Front Inflation Materials and the Extrusion Materials reflection settings are at 25%.

This would be a good time to save!

**Productivity Tip**: Here we have the elements coming together at this angle of view. If you need to move around to find other shapes I would save this angle of view so you can always come back to it. This means editing the camera not the object. Select the 3D Camera Rotate Tool in the toolbar and go in the options bar and locate the View Menu. Next to it you can see a small floppy disk icon. Click that and give the new camera view a name when prompted. Now you can use the camera tools to move around the subject to locate and reposition shapes; then simply choose your custom view in the menu to return to this angle of view.

**Step 16**: With the 3D elements in place let's now composite with other Photoshop elements. First thing is a cool nighttime city skyline that carries a similar color theme to the rest of the images. Drag and drop this image into the 3D layout and place it under the layer containing the 3D objects. To enhance the depth of field a bit more I added a small blur to the city image.

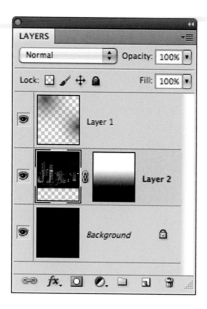

**Step 17**: Next, create a new blank layer just above the city image. All we are going to add here is a couple of Radial gradients using the same blue color of the text. This just enhances the background a bit and hints at a light source beyond the image bounds.

**Step 18**: Create another blank layer above this one and set the foreground color to white by pressing D. Using the same Radial Gradient Tool add some bigger gradients behind the 3D object to give a hint of light right behind it.

To give this gradient a more electric feel go into Layer Style panel and choose Outer Glow. In the Structure section set the blend mode to Hard Light and the Opacity to 100%. Click on the color swatch and change the RGB colors to R: 164, G: 104, B: 254. Lastly set the Size to around 85. This will give a nice glow but it needs something else. Hmmm…

**Step 19**: Since we are looking for a more electric look I am thinking some sparks will do the trick. We shall achieve this using a clever trick with layer styles. Before clicking OK, activate the Drop Shadow layer style. Drop Shadow? Yes. We actually need to add another outer glow but we only have one. However the drop shadow is merely a glow that you can offset. So we just won't offset it.

Go into the Structure section and set the blend mode to Dissolve. Click the color swatch and set the RGB numbers to R: 252, G: 206, B: 255. Click OK. Now set the Opacity to 3. This will have the appearance of small spark-like effects. Pretty cool!

**Step 20**: Now for the lightning elements on the cords. Create a new blank layer above the 3D layer and copy the same Electric Glow layer style and paste it to this new layer by simply right-clicking the Fx icon on the layer and choosing Copy Layer Style from the menu. Then just select the new layer, right-click the empty area again and choose Paste Layer Style. You will probably have to go into the Outer Glow and drop the size down a bit.

**Step 21**: Now select a soft edge brush in brush panel and set it to a relatively small size brush, around 5 pixels. Turn off all features that may be checked on in the Brush Options. However if you're using a pressure-sensitive tablet I would recommend checking on Shape Dynamics and setting the Size Control to Pen Pressure. This will help the lightning look more realistic.

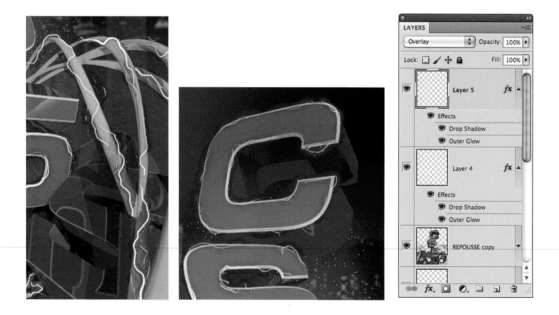

Now just start painting in the lightning elements around the yellow cords with very jagged strokes. Continue building the elements with varying length stokes; even add some around the letters. This part can be fun but be careful not to add too many.

**Step 22**: Duplicate this layer and press Command-A (Ctrl-A) to select all. Press Delete to remove everything on the layer. Notice, however, the layer style remains. This means anything added to this layer now will pick up the layer style. Next change the blend mode to Overlay. Then, using the same brush, continue to paint in reflections based on the strokes you already painted. You will also want to add strokes anywhere the yellow cords reflect in the letters. If you don't see the reflections go to the 3D panel and turn on Ray Traced Draft. Again don't go crazy, just enough to make it cool.

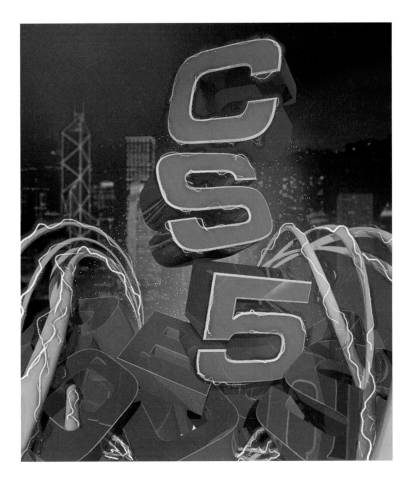

While this is just a small sampling of the numerous ways you can use Photoshop effects in conjunction with 3D effects, my hope here is that it gives you an idea what is possible with just a little experimentation. The best part is we did all of this without ever leaving Photoshop.

## 9.5. Cover Art Breakdown

Finally, in this chapter, I wanted do a little breakdown on the cover art — not necessarily a tutorial but rather just a description of how I approached and executed the concept, which, if you haven't guessed, was created entirely in Photoshop. This project, like so many design projects, went through several drafts before I finally settled on a good look, so I thought I would share some of the best practice techniques that I came up with while completing the final art.

### 9.5.1. Getting Started

Approaching this design project I knew that it needed to incorporate the Photoshop CS5 brand in a big way. So I started with a simple text layer of the letters CS5 in a font called Eurostile. Yes, I know, I used the same font in the last tutorial but it is a good font for 3D letters. When creating 3D letters it is a good idea to use really bold, simple-to-read letters. Try to avoid scripted fonts or fonts with serifs as these tend to be less readable and honestly look horrible in 3D.

With the text element sorted out I am ready to go ahead and start building the 3D environment. For that I am going to need a surface to set the 3D letters on and to reflect 3D elements. In this case the ground plane is merely made up of a gray layer fading to black. The lighter element in the middle will enhance the lighting once it's in the 3D environment. I use gray to start as a base to build the design and I can go back and change to a color later.

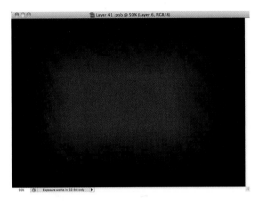

With these elements done I am ready to get started creating the 3D elements. I started by making the text a single 3D object using Repoussé. Since I knew I was going to be arranging the letters in different places, I went into the 3D menu to Repoussé and selected Split Repoussé Meshes. This splits up the letters but keeps them within the same 3D layer.

I then proceeded to merge these two 3D layers together into a single 3D layer. At this point the ground plane is parallel to the text so I needed to rotate the ground plane to be perpendicular to the letters. Then using the 3D mesh tools I moved the letters into position in the ground plane. The placement of the letters was a critical decision. I put the 5 a little more in the foreground because as this is the newest release of the creative suite I wanted to emphasize that more. I then tilted the overall object layout to add a bit more interest.

Now at this point I can see that just the letters aren't going to be enough. I need to add something to the background. Not wanting to go outside Photoshop I turned to the custom shape library and found an interesting leaf shape. On its own it's not a very interesting shape but with some creative placement it can become an interesting abstract element. So I converted the shape into a Repoussé object and then made a duplicate. I then merged the two shapes together with the main 3D layout and then used the 3D mesh tools to strategically place the shapes just behind the text.

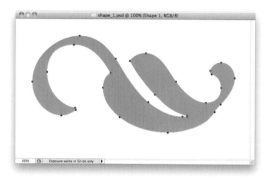

Here is an angle from above so you can see where I placed the shapes in relation to the letters.

Now here is a critical point that I touched on in the last lesson. Once I set the text and ground plane I really liked the angle at which I was viewing the art, and I was getting to the point now where I needed to start adding lights to the scene. When you add lights to a 3D scene in Photoshop they will be static; even if you use the 3D object rotate tools the object will change, but the lights will remain static. This results in the object's appearance changing as the lighting is different. To keep the lights in place in relation to the subject you will need to shift your view with the camera tools. This is very helpful when moving an object around in a 3D layer with multiple objects. You simply move the camera view around to see the art from a different angle, then use the object mesh tools to make adjustments where needed. You will need to first save the original camera angle view before you go moving the camera around; do this by selecting the Camera Tool in the toolbar then go to the options bar and you will see the View menu. Next to that you will see the small floppy disc icon. Click on this and enter a name for this angle when prompted. With the main view saved, you can now use the camera tools to move around the art making it easier to edit. To return to the main view just select it from the View menu.

Before I added the lights I needed to figure out a way to incorporate the Photoshop name in the layout. I finally decided to use a light, but I wanted it to have a Gobo light effect that shines a logo on a wall or floor. To achieve this I created a new blank layer and filled it with black, then converted it into

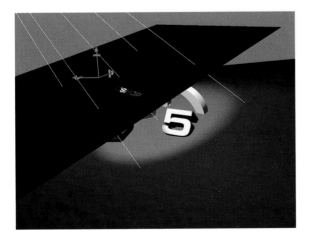

a 3D postcard and merged it with the rest of the 3D elements. The idea is to shine a light through this layer onto the ground plane. There first needs to be a hole through the plane. The hole is going to be the word Photoshop, so it needed to be a mask file that I created in the 3D panel in the Materials section.

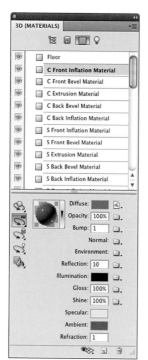

Notice in the last image on page 147 how the plane is placed above the rest of the 3D elements with the word Photoshop punched out of the plane. Notice the spotlight wireframe shows the light above the plane shining through down to the main surface plane. When rendered we will see the word Photoshop shining on the ground plane.

The next thing was to add the remaining lights to finish the scene. I ended up with a total of four spot lights on the entire scene including the gobo light. 3D lights are another aspect of 3D in Photoshop that you will want to really practice with. They can make or break a scene and they do require a little practice to master the positioning. There are several kinds of lights you can add but I have found that the spot lights offer the most dramatic effects. You can add multiple lights to a single scene and you can vary the color and intensity of each light.

Lights are also obvious critical elements for creating shadows and reflections. So with the lights in place I can use the 3D panel to vary the intensity of the reflections and shadows. The Reflections settings for each mesh surface are located in the Materials section of the 3D panel. This is helpful because you don't really want to have every surface reflect the same way. In reality if you wanted to lessen the reflection on a surface you would simply turn down the light or diffuse it. In the 3D world you can actually set how reflective a surface is going to be. Throughout the entire scene, almost every surface has a different setting for the reflection and the shadow.

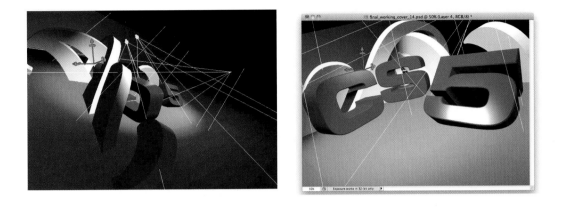

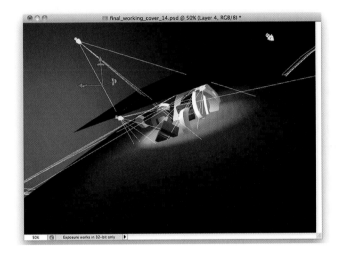

Of course, as these changes are being made we can see the lights on the surface but we cannot see the reflections or the shadows. That is because of the render mode. The default render mode is the Interactive Draft mode, which allows you to work with 3D faster, but in order to view any shadows or reflections you need to go into Ray Tracer mode. This is located in the Scene section of the 3D panel in the Quality menu. There are three options. Ray Traced Draft does a quick render that allows you to see the shadows and reflections so you can make changes if necessary. When Draft mode is selected you can click or press any button to pause the render; then when you make a change it will automatically start rendering again. It will continue to do this until you change the Quality setting back to Interactive Draft mode. Then you would use the Ray Traced Final when you are ready to do the final

render when you're finished. It might be a good idea to render at the end of the day as it will take a while depending on the subject. If you have the luxury of a second machine, then you can have it crunching on the render while you continue to work.

Now there is one last thing I wanted to mention that I added to this cover art but that ultimately did not make it in the final render. Did you know you can actually add depth of field to a 3D scene in Photoshop? Do this by clicking and holding on the Camera Tool in the toolbar to reveal all the camera tools. Select the 3D Zoom Camera Tool at the bottom. Look up in the Options to the far right and you will see settings for the Depth of Field, Blur and Distance. These settings are touchy so start small. Enter 3 in the Blur setting and you will notice the blur on the 3D object. However the focal point may not be where you want it to be. To change it just hold down the Option key (Windows: Alt) and click where you want the 3D object to be in focus. Then do a draft render to see how the blur looks. It's a great feature that can really add that one extra hint of realism. This is an extreme example as a Blur setting of 3 is a bit high, but it gives you a good idea of how it works. Pretty cool, huh?

So that is basically how I approached creating the cover art of this book. While 3D in Photoshop is still relatively new, you have to admit these features are pretty extraordinary with what they allow you to accomplish in just a few steps.

My goal, in this chapter, was to show you not only the cool things you can do with these new features, but also how you can work effectively with them. From here I will impart to you the same piece of advice I give to everyone: Experiment! Go and explore these features and really push them to see what you can achieve. As much as Photoshop has evolved over the past years, there is virtually nothing you can't do with a little practice and a spark of inspiration.

Experiment — be creative — have fun!

# CHAPTER 10

# Painting, Texturing and Lighting with Stephen Burns

With the introduction of 3D capabilities starting in CS3, concept artists had the potential to introduce 3D models into their concept scene. It was best at that stage of development to texture the 3D model in its native program and allow Photoshop to simply read what was already created. Then CS4 came along which made some great improvements in how well it handled 3D geometry. Its ability to use its painting tools directly on the 3D object was a feature that artists greatly appreciated, but even then there were limitations.

Now we are going to explore what are, in my humble opinion, some great improvements in CS5's 3D texturing engine.

Texturing infuses character into the 3D object to bring out the personality needed to tell a story. Without this your object is naked and lifeless. Texturing is an art within itself and some artists will specialize in just that. A great amount of time can be invested into this — days or weeks depending on the demands of the creative director.

**3D in Photoshop. DOI: 10.1016/B978-0-240-81377-6.10010-9**

**153**

Real-life objects absorb light to some degree and what we see is the results after absorption. If you look at objects around you, whether they are fabric, water, leaves or even a mountainous landscape, it is important to break down what we are seeing into their surface types. Basically, 3D programs identify and manipulate objects as several surface types by breaking them up into materials. For more information on materials, see Chapters 1 and 4.

Keep in mind that this chapter is written for the artist who has little or no knowledge of 3D creation; however there is the desire to add 3D content to their workflows, to introduce eye-catching effects as well as greater flexibility with their designs. We will accomplish this through the use of an online database that will provide quite a bit of the 3D content that we can use for our personal projects. Although we will provide a few companies for you to consider, we will focus on one online company that has created a plugin for CS5 that will import 3D objects directly into the 3D layers. The company is 3DVIA (www.3dvia.com).

We are going to illustrate a common compositing concept in this chapter. We will import a concept car from 3DVIA to use as the main character in our scene. We will illustrate it by showing it speeding through the wet streets of a downtown area of a city block that we will also download through 3DVIA database.

**Note**: This tutorial requires some basic knowledge of Photoshop tools such as the Clone Stamp, Transform, Various Shape Tools, Gradients and more. If you are not familiar with these tools, you should first learn these before proceeding.

Ok, let's start creating!

## 10.1. Importing 3D Using 3DVIA

We are now going to look at some possible online databases where you can download the 3D object that you require and import and texture it to your needs. There are a few companies for you to consider that use 3D content. Most have online databases where you would download the 3D object in your required format through their websites. Some of these include: 3D Via (www.3dvia.com), Artists 3D (http://artist-3d.com/), Quality 3D Models (www.quality3dmodels.com/), 3D Content Central (www.3dcontentcentral.com/) DAZ 3D (www.daz3d.com) and Content Paradise (http://www.contentparadise.com/) to mention a few.

The one that we will focus on for this tutorial is 3DVIA. 3DVIA is owned by Dassault Systems (www.3ds.com) which specializes in CAD based products. Seeing the need for an extensive 3D database similar to what Corbis & Getty Images has done for photography, Dassaut Sytems created 3DVIA. We will use their 3D importer plugin for Photoshop to import the models for this tutorial. You can find their plugin on 3DVIA's website at http://www.3dvia.com/products/3dvia-for-adobe-photoshop/ or on my personal website at http://www.chromeallusion.com/tutorials. html. Please download the plugin and install it. The plugins are designed to function on versions CS3 through CS5 so download and install the one that matches your version of Photoshop and let's begin the importing process.

We are going to create a scene with a concept car speeding through the wet streets of a downtown city.

**Note:** You can follow along with this tutorial by downloading the content files from http://www.chromeallusion.com/tutorials.html so look for the section titled **"3D IN PHOTOSHOP EXTENDED"**. Download and expand the zipped files into a folder titled "downloads" and we will refer to this for any content files that you will need for this tutorial. By the way, the 3D files used in this tutorial are included in the content files as well. So, let's download a 3D city and a sporty car through 3DVIA.

**Step 1**: Access the Import command (File > Import) and select "search 3DVIA" (Figure 10.1).

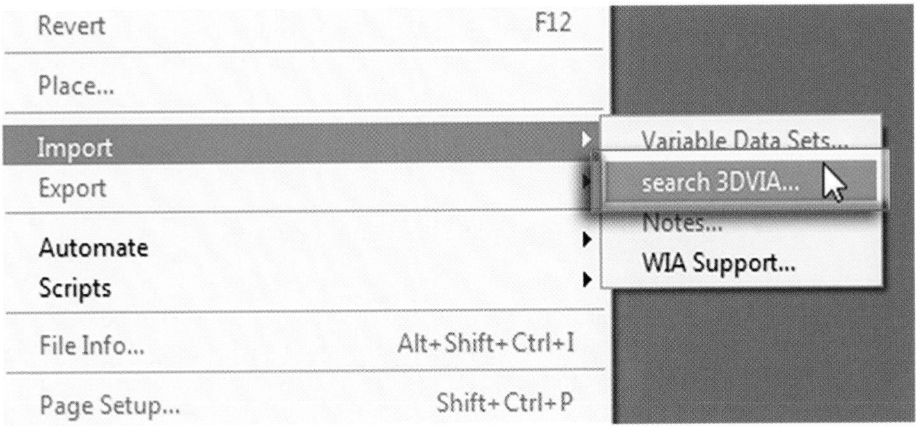

FIG 10.1 Access the Import command.

**Step 2**: The "search 3DVIA" importer will open the model search dialog box that will allow you to search by model type as well as by the name of the model. You will also be given options to search through the store where you will usually find some of the better models; however, I have found that the Community models are quite detailed. In this example the UCI Concept car is chosen (Figure 10.2).

Notice that the format of this model is 3D XML. This is a proprietary format by Dassault System's designed for a seamless transfer from their web based system (3DVIA) into Photoshop's 3D layers. After you have imported the concept car, browse through the database to acquire your city titled "City Block." We have provided both files for you in a PSD format so, if you like, access your downloads folder and open "skyscaper.psd" and "UCI Concept car Materials_AllCATPart 3D XML File.psd" (Figures 10.3 and 10.4).

FIG 10.2 Choose from the 3DVIA database.

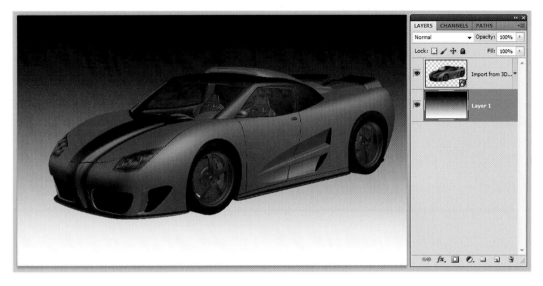

FIG 10.3 Open "UCI Concept car Materials_AllCATPart 3D XML File.psd."

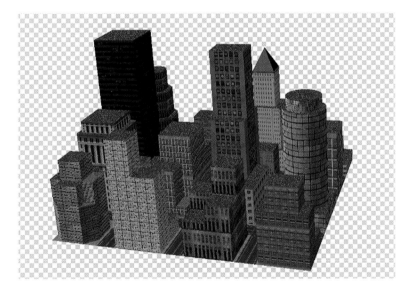

FIG 10.4 Open "skyscraper.psd."

## 10.2. Creating the Layout

Now we are going to position the 3D models to be in line with the concept of the car speeding through wet streets.

**Step 1**: Create a new document with the dimensions of 8" x 6" with 150 ppi resolution. This resolution is just for tutorial purposes so that we can work quickly together.

**157**

**Step 2**: Place both the car and the skyscraper objects in the new document. Each 3D object will occupy its own layer as shown in Figure 10.5.

**Step 3**: Access the 3D Mesh panel (Window > 3D) (Figure 10.6). Along the top of the panel click the first icon on the left to display the 3D Mesh options. On the bottom right of the panel click and hold on the icon on the far left to see the visibility options for the varied 3D components. Select "Show All" and instantly you can see outlines that represent 3D Axis, 3D Ground Plane, 3D lights and 3D Selection. This will help you to keep track of where things are as we navigate our scene to compose and texture it.

**FIG 10.5** Place the 3D objects into the new document.

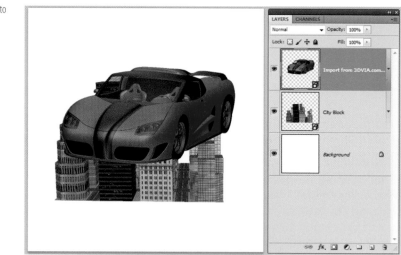

**FIG 10.6** View of the 3D Mesh panel.

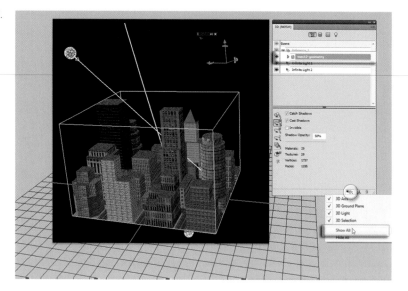

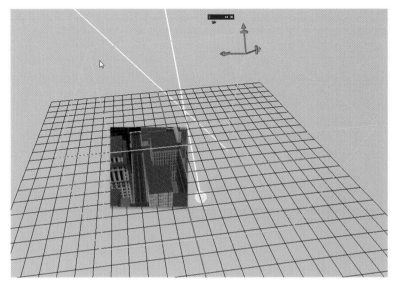

FIG 10.7 View of document zoomed out.

Zoom out of the document just to observe the changes to how we view our 3D space. CS5 will keep all 3D elements visual even beyond the borders of the document (Figure 10.7).

Now zoom in a little closer to get a better view of the streets. We will set up the scene for the car to be placed on one of the roads surrounded by the buildings (Figure 10.8).

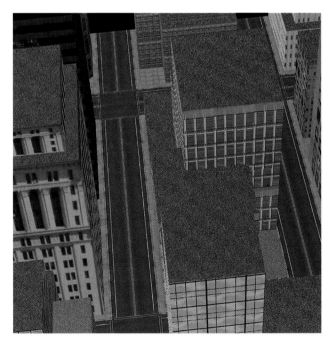

FIG 10.8 Get a closer view of the street.

**Note:** CS5 has the ability to merge both objects into a single layer using the Merge 3D Layers command so that both can be lit with the same light source, with the shadows and reflections affecting one another. However, third party models created by a community of artists are not always reliable. This could be due to how well the mesh of a 3D object was constructed, so to keep matters simple let's keep each object on its own 3D layer.

Make sure that the skyscraper layer is selected and navigate the Camera (N) so that it is close to street level with the front of the buildings in the background, as shown in Figure 10.9. Select the Camera Zoom option on the options bar. This is where we will set the focal length of the camera. To consolidate the field of view for both you will need to adjust the focal length of the camera toward a unified focal length so set the Focal Length to 100 for both objects. Now select the car layer and access the 3D navigation tools (K) and navigate the 3D object itself to be positioned over the street. Try to get something close to what you see in Figure 10.9.

**FIG 10.9** Compose the scene.

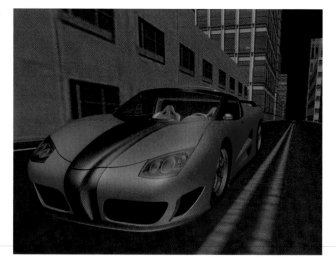

**Note**: As with many Photoshop tools, the Shift key can be used to limit interaction to one axis at a time. This will help you better control the interaction when getting used to the 3D tools.

**Step 4**: CS5 generally allows for the shadow of the 3D object to appear on the ground plane of the 3D model. But keep in mind that this is not always the case with third party 3D objects like the ones that we have just downloaded from 3DVIA. These models have been created by individuals and submitted to the website so, depending on the settings as well as the 3D application that created the objects, CS5 may or may not recognize the ground plane as in this particular case. So, to give our concept car a sense of placement on the ground plane, add a shadow on a separate layer beneath the car as shown in Figure 10.10. Change the layer's blend mode to Multiply and reduce the opacity a bit and let's continue on.

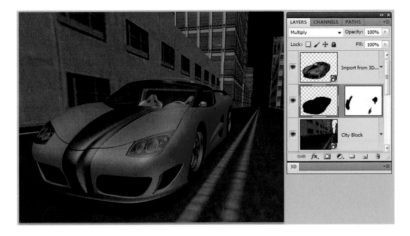

FIG 10.10 Add shadow for the car.

**Step 5**: Now let's add the sky to the background. This is done with gradients situated on their own layers; and initial light to darker blue is established on one layer. On top of that create a reddish gradient that falls off to 0% Opacity toward the top of the composition. Create another layer on top of the red gradient and create a dark blue to 0% Transparency toward the lower $^3/_4$ portion of the image. Use Figure 10.11 as a guide.

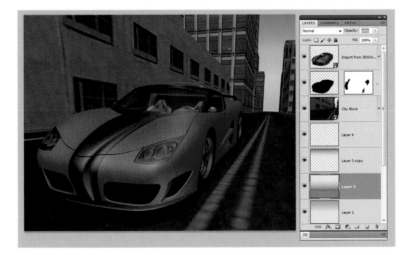

FIG 10.11 Add sky to the scene.

**Step 6**: Next, let's add some clouds to add some interest in the sky. Access the downloads folder and open the clouds.jpg and place it above the blue gradient. Resize and place them into the sky behind the skyscrapers and reduce the opacity to allow some of the sky colors to come through. In this example a duplicate is also applied and resized larger to imply depth (Figure 10.12).

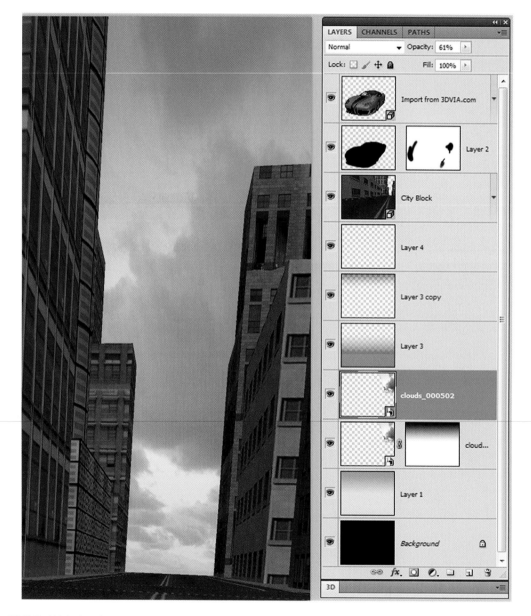

FIG 10.12 Add clouds to the scene.

**Step 7**: Now, focus on the layer titled "City Block" and take notice of the textures associated with it. If you place your cursor over the second one down, with "road straight" in the title, you will get a thumbnail view of the texture (Figure 10.13). Double-click this texture to edit it.

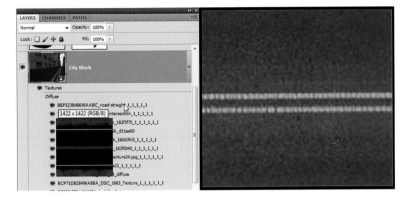

FIG 10.13 View road texture.

**Step 8**: By default, many of these textures will have a resolution of 72 ppi. To get more details we should redefine the texture to be a higher resolution. Change the Resolution in the Image Size properties (Image > Image Size) to 200 ppi instead and save the document (File > Save) (Figure 10.14).

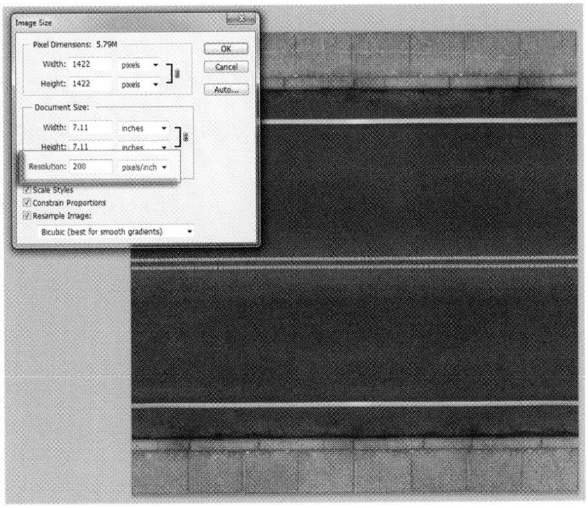

FIG 10.14 Change texture resolution to 200 ppi.

**Step 9**: When we resized the texture in Step 8, we have essentially inter-polated the image giving it a low resolution look. This is okay because we are now going to customize this texture at the higher resolution, starting with vector shapes.

FIG 10.15 Recreate lines using the
Vector Shape Tool.

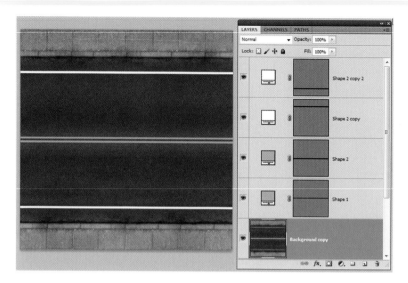

Recreate the orange and yellow paint guides using the rectangular vector
tools (U) (Figure 10.15). Simply match the original lines colors. In this
example, each vector shape is on its own layer. Select File > Save to see the
3D model update.

**Step 10**: Next, we will add a higher resolution image to add a concrete-like
texture to the street and sidewalk. Access your downloads folder and open
"concrete.jpg." Place the texture below the vector shapes as shown in
Figure 10.16. Select File- > Save to see the 3D model update.

FIG 10.16 Place "concrete.jpg" into
a new layer.

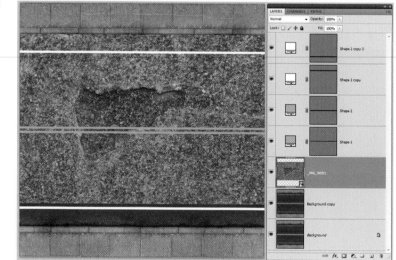

FIG 10.17 Use the clone tools to edit the texture.

**Step 11**: Use the Stamp Tool and the Patch Tool to get an even consistent texture (Figure 10.17). Select File > Save to see the 3D model update.

**Step 12**: The goal is to use the new texture to match the size of the texture information in the base image. So, use Free Transform (Ctrl-T/Cmd-T) and resize it, and then select it and create a new pattern as shown in Figure 10.18. Select File > Save to see the 3D model update.

FIG 10.18 Use the resized texture to create a patten.

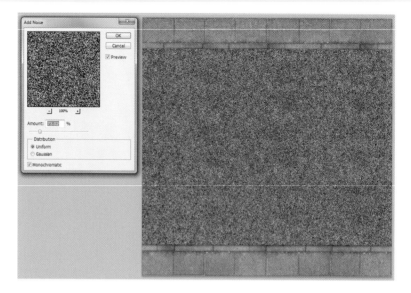

FIG 10.19 Fill layer with new pattern and add noise.

**Step 13**: Fill the layer with the newly defined pattern and add some noise (Figure 10.19). Select File > Save to see the 3D model update.

**Step 14**: Let's get the painted stripes to blend with the texture by changing the blend modes of the vector shapes to Overlay. To keep organized, place the painted shapes and texture into a new layer group titled "painted stripes." Use Figure 10.20 as a guide. Select File > Save to see the 3D model update.

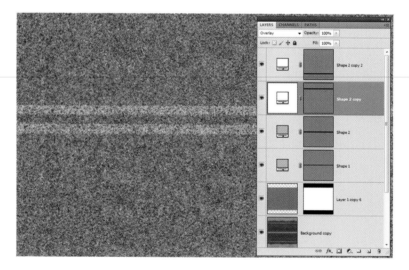

FIG 10.20 Change the blend modes of the vector shapes to Overlay.

**Step 15**: Create a new layer above the "painted stripes" layer group and change the blend mode to Multiply. Use a soft edge paint brush to paint black into the layer to give a feeling of ground-in dirt into the road (Figure 10.21). Select File > Save to see the 3D model update.

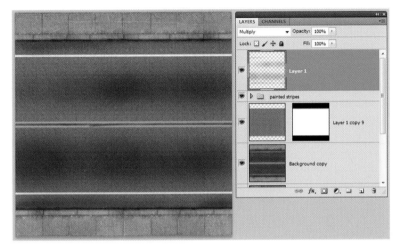

FIG 10.21 Apply dirt to the road.

**Step 16**: We are going to use another texture to add more detail to the street. Open "wall texture 002.jpg" (Figure 10.22).

Use the Patch Tool to make a seamless texture similar to what was done in Figure 10.17 (Figure 10.23). Select File > Save to see the 3D model update.

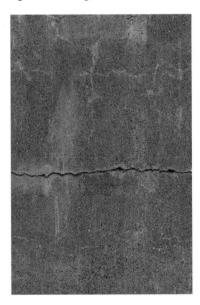

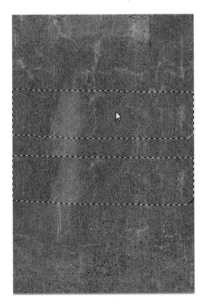

FIG 10.22 Open "wall texture 002.jpg."

FIG 10.23 Edit "wall texture 002.jpg" with the Patch Tool.

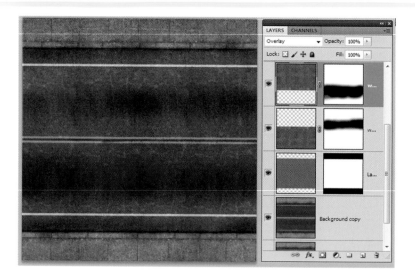

**FIG 10.24** Use layer masks to blend texture.

Change the blend mode to Overlay to increase the contrast so that the texture integrates with the road harmoniously underneath it (Figure 10.24). Place the texture to one side of the composition and duplicate it to cover the other side. Use layer masks to seamlessly blend the two. Select File > Save to see the 3D model update.

**Step 17**: The car will be driving along a rundown part of town and the roads will be in need of repair so let's further illustrate this. Select a portion of the "wall texture 002.jpg" that represents the long crack and place it in a new layer of the street texture. Change its blend mode to Hard Light and place it along the double yellow line (Figure 10.25). Select File > Save to see the 3D model update.

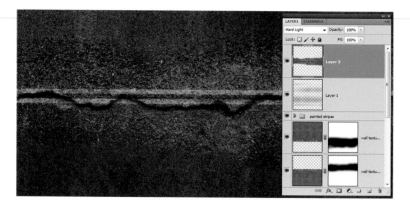

**FIG 10.25** Apply a cracked surface to the center of the street.

Use the layer mask to soften the edges to blend into the scene (Figure 10.26).

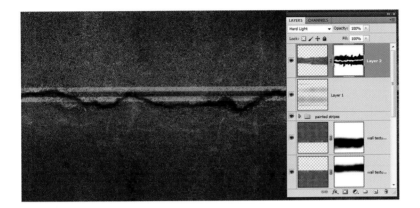

FIG 10.26 Use the layer mask to edit the texture.

**Step 18**: Finally, add another texture from the downloads folder titled "wall texture 003.jpg." Place this on its own layer and change its blend mode to Linear Light. This blend mode will help the highlights in the texture to jump out and since we want to have some control of the lighter tones reduce the Opacity to approximately 26% (Figure 10.27).

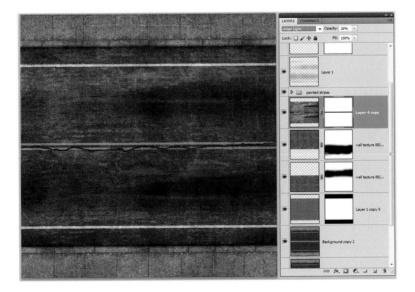

FIG 10.27 Apply additional texture to road.

Now, click Ctrl-S/Cmd-S to save the texture (Figure 10.28) and take a look at the 3D object to see the result.

**FIG 10.28** Save the texture.

## 10.3. Texturing the Walls of the Buildings

In this exercise we will add a little more character to the building.

**Step 1**: Select the City Block layer and access the sixth texture from the bottom that has the title of "texture 21" in it. You will see what is displayed in Figure 10.29.

FIG 10.29

**Note**: You can also use the Material Select Tool 🔧, and click on the canvas where this texture is. You will see the bounding box drawn around this material if you have the overlay turned on and the material should now be selected in your 3D Scene panel.

**Step 2**: Open the "wall texture 001.jpg" and place it above the background layer of the building. Use a layer mask to show through the windows from the base layer. To enhance the shadow details on the window sills use another layer with a Multiply blend mode and paint with black into the shaded areas (Figure 10.30). Select File > Save to see the 3D model update.

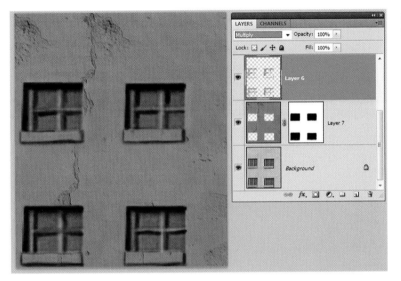

FIG 10.30 Add green wall and more intense shadow detail.

**Step 3**: Open the "wall texture 004.jpg" and place it above the "wall texture 001.jpg" layer (Figure 10.31). Use a layer mask again to show through the windows from the base layer. Change its blend mode to Hardlight and notice how well the details integrate. Select File > Save to see the 3D model update.

FIG 10.31 Add "wall texture 004. jpg" to enhance image.

**Step 4**: Let's add two more texture details to bring the wall to life. First, we will add some grunge detail to the wall. Open "wall texture 005.jpg" and set its blend mode to Darken. This dirties up the wall a bit giving a sense of age and neglect (Figure 10.32). Next, open and add the "wall texture 004.jpg" again as another layer and increase its contract using Curves. Change the blend mode to Overlay (Figure 10.33). Save the texture and let's go make changes to the lighting.

**FIG 10.32** Add "wall texture 005. jpg" to give the wall some grunge.

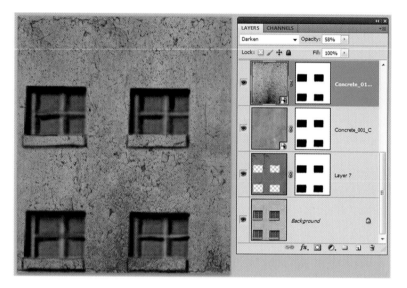

**FIG 10.33** Add "wall texture 004. jpg" and change the blend mode to Overlay.

# 10.4. Lighting the 3D model

One of the significant additions to the CS5 3D engine is the ability to use IBL (image based lighting). That means that you can take any photographic image and utilize its Color and Luminance properties to light the scene so that your models will actually look as if they were photographed within the same environment. For more information on image based lights, see Chapters 1 and 5. Let's start with lighting the car.

**Step 1**: Click on the "add new light" icon and select "New Image Based Lights". Now that the light has been added to the scene, all we need to do is select the image that it will use to light the model. If you select any light tool, take note that a 3D navigational sphere for the IBL light will be displayed for you to facilitate navigating the light.

**Note:** Although it is customary to add 360 degree panoramic HDR images, it is important to know that you can use any bitmap image; that is what we will do in this situation.

Inside the 3D Lighting panel click on the add image icon that is next to the "Image" title located below the color swatch. Navigate to your downloads folder and select "ibl lightsource.jpg." This is the merged imagery of the background scene as shown in (Figure 10.34).

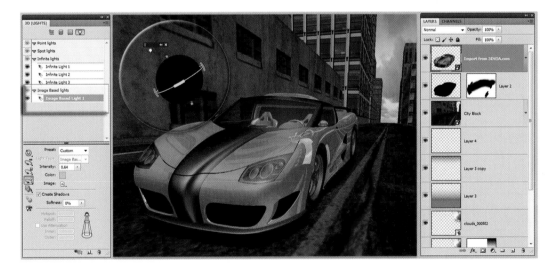

FIG 10.34 Add image based lighting to the car.

**Step 2**: It is a good idea to match the ambient light in the scene. If you like, select any color so that you can see how this feature will affect the car; however the reddish bluish horizon was chosen in this example (Figure 10.35).

FIG 10.35 Select the ambient color for the car.

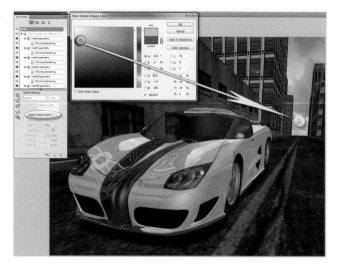

**Step 3**: Let's take a look at the actual surface properties on the concept car. The 3D Materials panel will display all of the separate 3D surfaces that are attached to this model. As you can see there are quite a few (Figure 10.36). Through the 3D Materials panel you can select each 3D mesh and view its surface. In this example "mesh643-geometry" is chosen and below is its surface titled "Gris_argent_Rendering."

**Note:** These titles were the originals given when the car was created in its native 3D program. However, you can change them by double-clicking on their titles and typing in the new name.

FIG 10.36 Take a look at the surface properties.

**Step 4**: Now we are going to add some ambient lighting to the City Block so select that layer and this time choose a more bluish color within the clouds (Figure 10.37). Since this portion of the buildings is mostly in shadow we will allow it to be dominated by the bluish temperature that often dominates shadow regions of a photographic image.

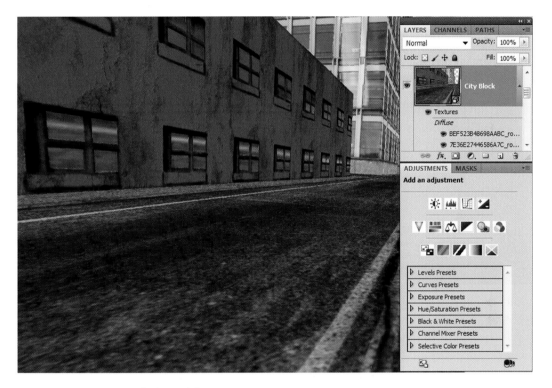

FIG 10.37 Select the ambient color for the City Block.

Next we will add a wet looking surface to the street.

## 10.5. Adding the Wet Look to the Street

The car will kick up water as it is speeding through the streets. But first let's give the road a wet look. Essentially we are going to affect the Reflection properties of the street. Let's get started.

**Step 1**: Make sure that the City Block layer is chosen. With the 3D Materials panel open select the material for the street which is "GraphicMaterial-32."

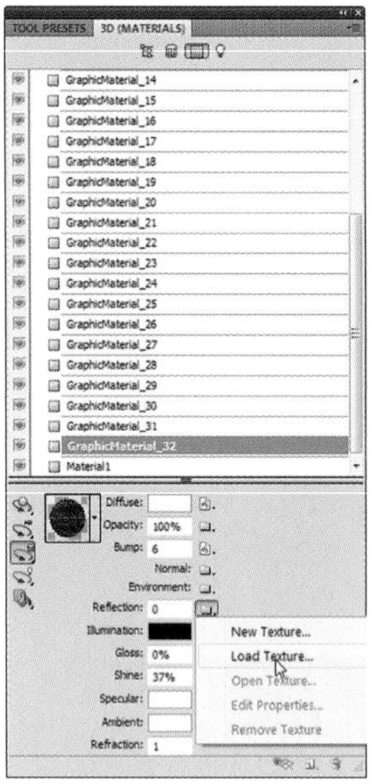

**Note**: Materials can also be selected using the Select Material Tool found in the Material Tools slot on the 3D panel 🔲 . From the Reflection texture popup menu, choose Load In A New Texture as shown in Figure 10.38.

Next, navigate to your downloads folder and select "ground reflection. jpg." We are using a B&W image to define the reflective characteristics of the model. The brighter the tones the more reflective the object will be and the darker the tones the less reflective it will be (Figure 10.39).

Adjust the Reflection intensity to 80% so that you can get a feel to what this texture is doing to the surface of the street (Figure 10.40).

Next, adjust the Reflection intensity to 30%. This is more of what we are looking for (Figure 10.41).

**FIG 10.38** Load in a new texture for the Reflection properties.

**FIG 10.39** Use "ground reflection.jpg" for the Reflection properties.

**FIG 10.40** Adjust the Reflection intensity to 80%.

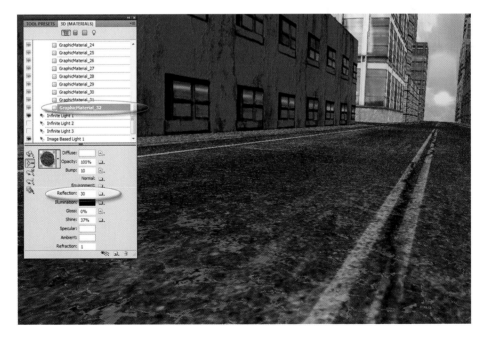

**FIG 10.41** Play with the Reflection intensity from 80% to 30%.

## 10.6. Adding Localized Bump and Reflective Characteristics

Now we are going to finish up a few details to the cityscape behind the car. We will add localized bump and reflective details to the buildings as well as the setting between the buildings.

**Step 1**: Turn off the visual aspect of the car temporarily to have less distraction on the city (Figure 10.42).

**Step 2**: Just as you did in Figure 10.38 you are going to find the surface in the 3D Materials panel for the tallest building in the rear (GraphicMaterial_10). Again, you can use the Select Material Tool to select it directly on canvas; once selected, load the file "build reflective map.jpg" into its Reflection map (Figure 10.43).

This image is the B&W version of the original color image. The window regions were selected with the Polygonal Selections Tool and filled with white on a separate layer. The background layer was then filled with black. This ensures that only the windows will have reflective properties.

FIG 10.42 Hide the car to focus on the city.

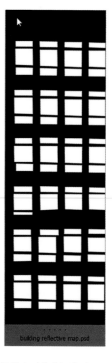

FIG 10.43 Load "build reflective map. jpg" into the Reflection properties of the "GraphicMaterial_10" surface.

**Step 3**: We will create the bump map in a similar way. Figure 10.44 is a B&W version of the color map. Just like the reflective map, the white areas will rise to display peaks and the black areas have no effect. Now, load "building 2 bump map.jpg" into the Bump map of GraphicMaterial_10.

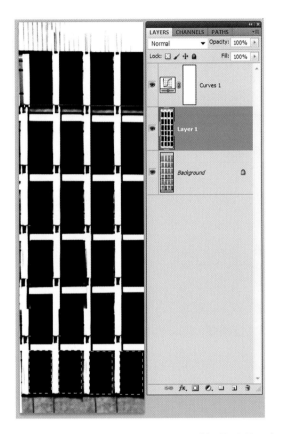

FIG 10.44 Load "building 2 bump map.jpg" into the Bump properties of the "GraphicMaterial_10" surface.

In our 3D Scene panel (Window > 3D) access the Quality drop-down menu and select Ray Traced Final to see the results. You will initially see a square grid pattern moving across our image. This is simply making several passes to improve the render by minimizing noise. You should now see the reflections from the surfaces of the neighboring building only within the glass windows as a result of the reflection map. Also, the white colored supports appear to rise forward, which is the white colors in that region of the bump map (Figure 10.45).

**Step 4**: Now do the exactly same thing to the building in the foreground for "GraphicMaterial_8" and use "building_reflect 1.jpg" for the reflection map and "building 1 bump map.jpg" for the bump. Adjust the intensity sliders to your liking. You should have something similar to Figure 10.46. Finally, to add some last minute feature that will hold our interest between the foreground and the background, place the "sunset.jpg" below the City layer and position it so that the sun is positioned between the buildings (Figure 10.46).

**FIG 10.45** Render scene with Ray Traced Final to see the end result.

**FIG 10.46** Load "building 1 bump map.jpg" into the Bump properties and "building_reflect 1.jpg" for the Reflection properties of the "GraphicMaterial_8" surface. Add the sunset to the background.

## 10.7. Adding Depth of Field and the Splash

We are about to do something really fun and add the splash that is caused by the speeding car. In addition we will use the new DOF (Depth Of Field) features in the Camera Zoom Tool to limit the focus on the main character, which is the concept car.

**Step 1:** Let's start with the Car Layer to apply the new DOF feature. Select the 3D Zoom Camera Tool. On the options bar there are two variables that we are interested in. One is the "DOF Blur," which establishes the strength of the blur and the other is "Distance," which will set the plane of focus. In this example the Distance is set so that the rear of the car begins to blur into the distance (Figure 10.47). With the 3D Zoom Camera Tool you can Opt/Alt click on the rear of the car to set that as the focal plane (distance parameter in the options bar).

**Step 2:** Do the same thing for the City Layer but set the Distance so that the rear of the image is blurred and the foreground is more in focus (Figure 10.48). Also apply some Gaussian Blur (Filter > Blur > Gaussian Blur) to the sunset to honor our chosen depth of focus.

**Step 3:** A brush is created to start the initial stage of the splash. Figures 10.49—10.51 show the brush properties that were used to create the brush for the splash.

FIG 10.47 Set the DOF Blur and Distance to blur the rear of the car.

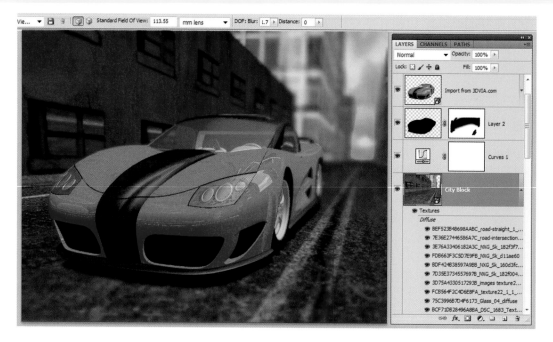

FIG 10.48 Set the DOF Blur and Distance to blur the rear of the car.

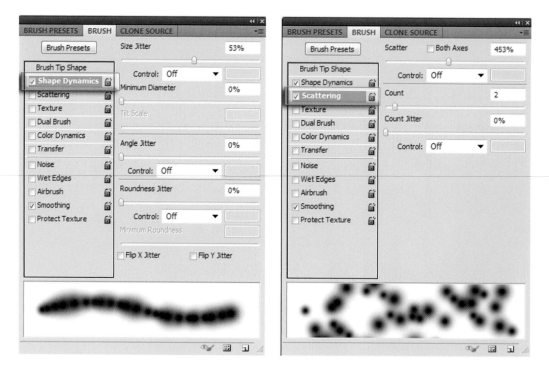

FIG 10.49 Shape Dynamic applied to Size Jitter.

FIG 10.50 Scatter and Count applied to brush.

FIG 10.51 Foreground and Background Jitter applied to Color Dynamics.     FIG 10.52 Apply the paint technique to a separate layer.

**Step 4**: Apply a purplish color for the foreground color and a dark blue for the background color. These two colors reflect the two extreme ambient light colors in the scene. Now apply the paint effect to a separate layer above the car. Use Figure 10.52 as a guide.

**Step 5**: To get the splash started give the paint some Motion Blur (Fillers > Blur > Motion Blur). A distance of 34 is used and leave the angle at "0" (Figure 10.53).

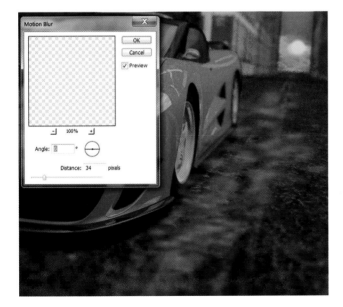

FIG 10.53 Apply Motion Blur with a distance of 34.

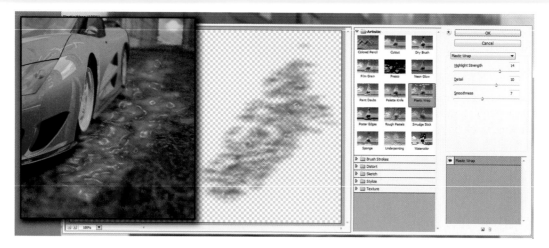

FIG 10.54 Apply Plastic Wrap filter.

**Step 6**: We will now give this paint stroke the glossy properties of water to apply the Plastic Wrap filter (Filters > Artisic > Plastic Wrap) as shown in Figure 10.54. Experiment with the settings till you find something to your liking.

**Step 7**: Now apply Motion Blur (Filters > Blur > Motion Blur), again with a greater distance (Figure 10.55). Now we have our initial splash.

FIG 10.55 Apply Motion Blur.

**Step 8**: Duplicate the splash to add a stronger effect. Then give it a drop shadow underneath to show depth from the ground. Also, to further harmonize the colors in the overall scene use a Radial gradient to add yellow to the sunset and a bluish hue to the foreground (Figure 10.56). Now it's time to render the car with ray tracing. In the 3D Scene panel (Window > 3D) select the scene slot on the scene graph area, and under the Quality drop-down menu select "Ray Traced Final." You should see that the reflections in the windows are now rendered.

FIG 10.56 Duplicate the splash layer and add gradient to harmonize color in the scene.

**Step 9**: Duplicate the car layer and change it to a Smart Object (right-click on layer > Convert to Smart Object). Add a Motion Blur with the Angle set to 70 degrees. Here the Distance is set to 41 but you can experiment with this to get a look you like. This gives the car a sense of motion and up and down movement (Figure 10.57).

FIG 10.57 Apply Motion Blur to get sense of bumpy up and down movement.

**Step 10**: Edit the mask of the Smart Filter so that the Motion Blur is mostly applied to the rear of the car instead of the front end. In addition, create an additional layer above the car and fill it with 50% gray. Add to this gray layer a Lens Blur (Filter Render > Lens Flair) and then change the blend mode to Hard Light to make the gray pixels transparent — leaving only the lens flair. Place the flare over the headlights to accentuate the glare (Figure 10.58).

FIG 10.58 Apply Lens Flare to headlights.

With a little more enhancements to the headlights as well as a light spill onto the street (separate layer set to Overlay with white added to the street), Figure 10.59 shows the final render.

I really do hope that you enjoyed this chapter. For more information on myself and my art please go to www.chromeallusion.com

FIG 10.59 Final results.

# CHAPTER 11

# Creating Lenticulars with Russell Brown

Ever go to a movie theater and notice a poster that changes views and/or appears to have depth when seeing it from different angles? That is what a lenticular image is. Lenticular images are a form of 3D stereo imagery resulting from combining multiple views (at least two) of a single image. This image is interlaced and matched to a lenticular lens or frame to display the visual 3D effect. Originally used mostly in novelty items, lenticular prints are now being used as a marketing tool to show products in motion and 3D. It is an element that is easier to add to your creative design now that Photoshop Extended has the ability to create and print these images.

Included in this book is an insert of a lenticular image that gives an illusion of depth. This chapter will cover basic techniques, useful information and best practices on how to get started with creating a lenticular image.

**Note**: Some of the tutorials covered in this chapter are taken directly from Russell Brown's website on Lenticular Imaging, with a few new additions. For a video tutorial on some of these techniques, visit http://www.russellbrown.com/3D.html

**3D in Photoshop. DOI: 10.1016/B978-0-240-81377-6.10011-0**

## 11.1. Getting Started

### 11.1.1. Equipment and Software

Creating lenticulars requires proper setup of your images, proofing (optional) and finally printing a lenticulated file to be used with a lens or frame and/or in some cases printed directly onto a lens. For this chapter, you will need to have the following basic equipment to get started.

- Adobe Photoshop CS4 or CS5 Extended
- Canon, Epson, or HP desktop inkjet printer
- High gloss, quick drying printing paper
- Lamination equipment or send prints directly to http://snapily.com, a lenticular printing service
- 3D red blue anaglyphic glasses (optional for proofing).

## 11.2. Basic Lenticular Workflow

This section will walk you through an example on how to create a lenticular in Photoshop Extended. It is a good place to start to familiarize yourself with best practices and new concepts in creating lenticulars. Open up the short animation that shows the final lenticular of this Double Identity movie poster found on the accompanying website for this book or http://www.russellbrown.com/3D.html.

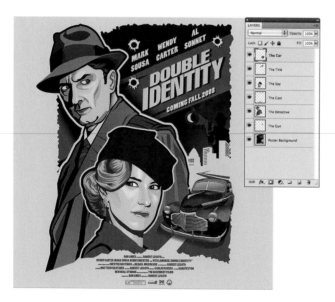

**Step 1**: Open the image "Double_-Identity_Poster75dpi.psd" so we can start to analyze how files need to be prepared for a 40 lpi (lines per inch) lenticular lens (Figure 11.1). We recommend starting with a 40 lpi lenticular lens as it is the easiest to work with. Microlens has excellent information on how to choose the right lpi for the particular project you are interested in. Visit http://www.microlens.com for more in depth information.

FIG 11.1 Double Identity poster split into layers where each layer will have a separate depth assigned to it.

**Setting Up Layers for Depth**

**Step 2**: Click through each layer and that each layer contains an element that will have a different depth applied. Further, the layer stack is set up so that the element that will be closest to the viewer is on top and the element that is farthest from the viewer will be in the background. For example, the layer "The Title" is the element that has the greatest depth from the background and is, therefore, closest to the viewer.

**Setting up image size**

**Step 3**: The final image of this project is on an 8" × 10" lenticular. However, the working file is set at 10" × 10" (Image > Image Size to view document dimensions). There is an additional 1" padding on each side for the width. This is because through the process of *interlacing* your image for a lenticular, you will introduce parallax in order to achieve the 3D effect (Figure 11.2). Because of parallax, you end up viewing more of the scene than you do when looking at it through a single lens and therefore you will need more space to accommodate for this camera motion. Interlacing is the process of breaking up an image into interlaced lines so that it can be aligned with a lenticular lens to create the effect of 3D.

FIG 11.2 Interlaced layer (Double_Identity_Lenticular.psd)

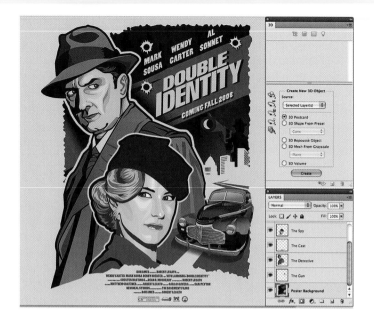

FIG 11.3 Covert each layer into a 3D postcard from the 3D Scene Panel.

### Convert to Postcard

**Step 4**: Select the "Poster Background" layer and convert it to a 3D postcard (3D > New 3D Postcard From Layer). You can also run this from the 3D Scene panel. Under the Source, select Selected Layer, check 3D Postcard and then hit Create (Figure 11.3).

**Note**: If you notice a color shift at this step, make sure that the document color profile matches that of the working space (Edit > Convert to Profile).

**Step 5**: Repeat Step 4 for each layer.

### Setting Depth of Layers

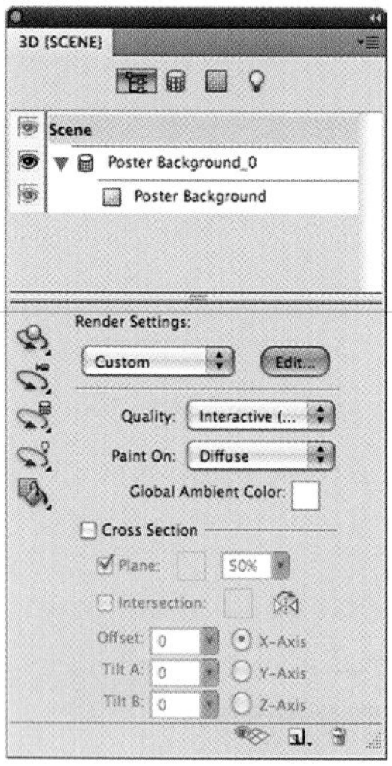

**Step 6**: Double-click "Poster Background" 3D layer. Clicking on any 3D layer will open up the 3D Scene panel (Figure 11.4). From the Scene filter of the 3D Scene panel click on the Edit button next to the Render Settings drop-down menu.

At the bottom of the 3D Render Settings dialog, select the last checkbox that enables stereo rendering (Figure 11.5). Set the Parallax to 30 and the Focal Plane to −80. Parallax is the distance between stereo cameras; a greater value enhances the depth between each of the layers. We recommend using a Parallax of 30 for 2D layered projects like this (optimum range of 15−30). A Focal Plane of "0" is the point of true focus; a negative value will push the layer back and a positive value will pull the layer forward. Here you can visualize how your image looks with an anaglyphic (red/blue) 3D effect.

FIG 11.4 3D Scene Panel invoked from double-clicking any 3D layer thumbnail.

## Proofing with Red/Blue Glasses (optional)

**Step 7**: With Red/Blue selected for the Stereo Type, put on your red/blue glasses and view the differences in depth effect created by altering the focal plane value.

FIG 11.5 3D Render Settings dialog set to view 3D layer as a Red/Blue stereo image.

## Creating the Lenticular — interlacing

**Step 8**: At the bottom of the 3D Render Settings dialog set the Stereo Type to Vertical Interlaced (Figure 11.6). Make sure that the lenticular spacing is set to 40 lpi (default value), Parallax 30 and Focal Plane −80.

FIG 11.6 3D Render Settings dialog set to view 3D layer as a vertically interlaced lenticular image.

**Step 9**: Select the layer "The Gun" and open up the Render Settings dialog. Change Stereo Type to Vertical Interlaced and set all values as you did in Step 9, except change the Focal Plane to −60. This will pull this layer forward from the background layer (plane).

**Step 10**: Select the layer "The Detective" and repeat the previous step but this time set the Focal Plane to −20.

**Step 11**: Select the layer "The Car" and repeat the previous step but this time set the Focal Plane to −10.

**Step 12**: Select the layer "The Cast" and repeat the previous step but this time set the Focal Plane to −5.

**Step 13**: Select the layer "The Spy" and repeat the previous step but this time set the Focal Plane to 0. This will set this layer to be the sharpest layer in focus. <OK>

**Step 14**: Select the layer "The Title" and repeat the previous step but this time set Focal Plane to 60. This will bring the title layer to the front and closest to the viewer.

**Prepare the Lenticular for Print**

**Step 15**: Select the Crop Tool and set the width to 8" and the height to 10". Set the resolution to the target resolution default depending on the type of printer you are using. Set the resolution to 600 ppi for HP printers, 720 ppi for Epson printers, and 600 ppi for Canon printers.

**Step 16**: Select the Crop tool and in the options bar select the option Hide. Click and drag over the image and position the crop out the extra edges. Hit Enter key or checkmark in options bar to crop the image.

**Step 17**: Check that the image is set to be at the target resolution, in this case 600ppi. Open up the Image Size dialog to verify. It is important to set up the best resolution and quality for this project.

**Print and Laminate to Lenticular Lens**

**Step 18**: Print your file and then take your 40 lpi lens and align it until you see the best depth effect. This might take a while to align perfectly so make sure you slide the image horizontally until the image looks just right and then laminate the lens onto the print.

**Note**: Snapily provides a great service for printing to lenticulars: http://pro.snapily.com/ From this site, you can directly upload your Photoshop layered files for professional quality printing of lenticulars.

# PART IV

# Appendices

# Appendix A
# File Formats

Adobe Photoshop Extended allows import of OBJ, COLLADA, KMZ, 3DS, and U3D files. It allows export of OBJ, COLLADA, KMZ and U3D files. 3DS is not included in the export because it is not a good format to use for interchange due to its limitations for geometry structure. In this appendix we will give a brief overview of each format with its capabilities, and what it's future is. The chart below illustrates the specific differences in each of the formats.

## OBJ

The OBJ file format is a text file format, so you can edit OBJ files in a text editor. It was originated by Wavefront Technologies, which no longer exists as a separate company. OBJ files only have geometry in them with associated

Table A.1   * Cameras and animations are not supported on U3D export (only import)

|  | OBJ | 3DS | U3D | DAE | KMZ |
|---|---|---|---|---|---|
| Cameras |  | x | x * | x | x |
| Lights |  | x | x | x | x |
| Animation |  | x | x * | x | x |
| Shaders |  |  |  | x | x |
| Single File |  |  | x |  | x |
| N-Sides | x |  | x | x | x |
| Open Standard |  |  | x | x |  |
| Mesh Compression |  |  | x |  |  |
| Text-Based | x |  |  | x | x |
| Diffuse | x | x | x | x | x |
| Bump | x | x | x | x | x |
| Opacity | x | x | x | x | x |
| Shininess | x | x | x | x | x |
| Self Illumination | x | x | x | x | x |
| Reflection | x | x | x | x | x |
| Environment | x | x | x | x | x |
| Normal |  |  |  | x | x |

materials. They do not have animation, lighting or cameras. It also supports NURBS surfaces – although Photoshop does not support the loading of NURBS. If the object has materials it will also have a .mtl file which contains the material description. This format is in use by many companies and most 3D tools import and export OBJ files so you can use it as a geometry interchange format if you wish. Going forward, OBJ is not an evolving format. Its specification is done and there is no new development being done on it.

Photoshop supports most of the OBJ format. We do not support the group tags as many people use it to create a hierarchy in the file. We have found through testing that the g tag is often used for naming and not grouping so trying to support this tag is like making a guess at what the user intended to do.

One version of the spec can be found at: http://www.martinreddy.net/gfx/3d/OBJ.spec although there isn't really an official specification for it.

## 3DS

3DS is a binary format, which means you can't edit it directly. The 3DS format is owned and developed by Autodesk. It is a proprietary format and there is no official spec available for it. Many people over the years have deduced the pieces of the format and have made loaders for it. Many of the blocks within 3DS are only known to Autodesk. 3DS has most of the capabilities you would need for your 3D models including geometry, materials, cameras, lights, and animation. It is a very popular format and since it is so old there are thousands of existing models. 3DS has no new development being done on it.

Photoshop supports the major portions of a 3DS file including geometry, instancing, animation tracks (the ones we know about), lights, cameras, and materials. We currently do not support morph targets, 3D path and curve objects, camera and light targets, or fog.

There are many sites on the internet that keep a library of 3DS files or just have samples for download. Because of the sheer number of files available in this format it is very difficult to say that they will all load properly in any 3D program. If you have problems loading one, try loading it into another program you might have and then try exporting it to COLLADA if you can. This may help if you are unable to load the file in Photoshop as 3DS.

## COLLADA and KMZ

COLLADA is an xml style format and you can edit it with any text editor. KMZ is a zip file that contains a COLLADA file along with its associated texture files and other documents meant to be used in Google Earth. Photoshop also reads this information and stores the Google Earth geographical positioning information. COLLADA is controlled by Khronos technologies and is an open standard that many companies contribute to. It is in active development and has been undergoing many changes in its first few versions. It contains all the types of information you need to have a complete 3D scene including geometry, materials, cameras, lights, animation, physics and shaders. Therefore COLLADA is a very good format to use for 3D interchange and many companies use it this way. A typical pipeline for game companies is to pass around COLLADA files. Most of the major 3D tools import and export COLLADA now with more and more smaller tools picking it up as well. Photoshop is trying to make this the format of choice for our users because it has so many capabilities.

Photoshop supports a good amount of what COLLADA can capture. We currently do not support bones and skinning in Photoshop but we have taken the time to try and preserve this information from the COLLADA file. If you have a skinned model in COLLADA and you bring it into Photoshop you will only see the base frame of geometry when it loads up. If you change anything in the file and then export it back to COLLADA we will take the data we preserved from the file and put it back. This should help minimize any problems of losing your information coming out of Photoshop and is another reason why we suggest you try to use COLLADA as the exchange format of choice. COLLADA is also the only format that supports all the map types Photoshop can use as well as user-generated ones. We also do not support the shaders and COLLADAFX information but we try to preserve that information as well.

COLLADA also has a Physics specification that is used in mostly gaming applications. Photoshop does not parse any of this data or preserve it in any way.

As of the printing of this book, COLLADA is now working on the 1.5 spec and, as the format evolves, Photoshop will take advantage of what we think is useful for our users.

The COLLADA spec can be found at: http://www.khronos.org/collada/

# U3D

U3D is a binary format. It is primarily used by CAD companies because of its ability to compress geometry. Intel was the originator of the format and it is now an open standard.

U3D contains most of the capabilities for a complete 3D scene but leaves out some of the specific texture types. U3D is an ECMA standard but new development has not taken place on it since 2007 when the last spec was produced. U3D is the format that Adobe uses in Acrobat 3D, and many other programs also export PDFs with U3D models as well.

Photoshop supports most of what U3D supports. There are a few map types that U3D does not have that Photoshop uses. U3D only supports one specular map whereas Photoshop supports specular intensity and specular exponent maps. U3D also does not support normal maps.

The U3D spec can be found at:

http://www.ecma-international.org/publications/standards/Ecma-363.htm

# Appendix B
## Interoperability and Limitations

In general, we advise that Photoshop be the last step, or one of the last steps, in your production workflow since Photoshop has advanced rendering capabilities as well as the ability to do all of your touch-up work without having to leave the application. If you do plan on using multiple products to accomplish your work then we would advise that you use COLLADA as your main interchange format. Right now it is the one format we use that can represent most of the items we need to support on import or export. Photoshop CS5 is currently compatible with the 1.4.1 spec for COLLADA. If you use Autodesk 3D Studio Max or Maya you should get a copy of the ColladaMax or ColladaMaya plugins if you want to have a smooth workflow with Photoshop. These plugins will make your output out of these programs much more compatible than using the built in exporters. Most 3D programs now output and input COLLADA files so programs like DAZ 3D, Poser, SoftImage, Cinema 4D, etc. should all work well.

**Note**: If you are using Sketchup from Google you should be aware that the default settings on the export to COLLADA dialog are not compatible with Photoshop CS5. You need to make sure the checkbox named "Preserve component hierarchies" is not checked. Otherwise, Photoshop will not be able to parse the file. If you download any files from Google 3D warehouse you will need to watch out for this as well. If you have a problem loading the file in Photoshop, bring it back into Sketchup and export with that setting turned off and this should fix the problem.

If you want to eventually include your file in an Acrobat document you should export it as a U3D file. All you need to do is to open up Acrobat Professional and use the Create PDF from File command and then add your U3D file.

If you would like to import your file into Google Earth you should export it as a KMZ file.

OBJ is useful if you are just doing model transfers as it does not contain animation, lights or cameras. Because it is such a simple format it is usually very reliable for model interchange.

# Index